futureDJs

How to DJ

A guide to DJ-ing
and electronic music
by Austen Smart,
Scott Smart and
Tom Dent

Audio Included

MW00653885

FABER *ff* MUSIC

First published in 2020 by
Faber Music Limited
Bloomsbury House
74–77 Great Russell Street
London WC1B 3DA

Samples by **Cr2 records**

Audio created by **FutureDJs**, featuring **Hugo Mansion**

Design + illustrations: **Lisa Gifford Design**
All equipment drawings are based on Pioneer DJ equipment

Pioneer Dj

Contributors:
DJ Mark One and **Mr Switch**

Printed in Turkey by **Imago**

ISBN10: 0–571–54061–9
EAN13: 978–0–571–54061–7

To buy Faber Music publications or to find out about
the full range of titles available please contact
your local music retailer or Faber Music sales enquiries:

Faber Music Limited
Burnt Mill, Elizabeth Way
Harlow CM20 2HX

t: +44(0) 1279 82 89 82
f: +44(0) 1279 82 89 83

sales@fabermusic.com I fabermusicstore.com

Contents

About FutureDJs

In 2016, we set out on a mission to transform how children experience music at school. The vision: to make music accessible to all young people and provide the world's best electronic music education. Now, thanks to an incredibly passionate team, DJ-ing is on the National Curriculum, decks are a musical instrument, our DJ course is accredited and there are FutureDJs tutors all over the country teaching students how to DJ, and still every day the tempo increases!

Everyone at FutureDJs has a profound love of music and all care deeply about young people having the chance to enjoy a music education. We do this by teaching relevant, engaging and accessible courses that help students take their learning to the next level.

We believe that learning and taking part in music boosts a young person's mental wellbeing and can give them the confidence they need to flourish in all walks of life. Learning how to DJ can also help students develop their communication, problem-solving and critical-thinking skills. By developing these skills, students will be well equipped for a future working in any industry and, at the very least, they will have opened a gateway to a whole new world of electronic music, including DJ-ing, music production, improvisation, composition and performance.

We reach out to the DJ-ing community for knowledge and insight from industry professionals right across the spectrum of electronic dance and traditional music.

In short — we're remixing music education.

If you want to know more, visit **futuredjs.org** or get in touch with the team at **interest@futuredjs.org**

Acknowledgement

Sincere thanks to Mark Blundell (DJ Mark One), for his wisdom and co-operation; Tony Culverwell (aka Mr Switch) for our chance meeting and subsequent discussions and teamwork; Dr Pete Dale for his support from the outset; Faber Music, for facilitating a project of passion; the UK Pioneer DJ team, in particular Martin Dockree and Mary Jong, for their belief in our vision for the company before it had even been formed; friends and family for their endless encouragement and support; the FutureDJs team for their hard work and commitment and the FutureDJs tutors out there in the practice rooms, delivering lessons to students in schools.

Foreword by Dr Pete Dale

Senior lecturer in Music and Sound

What is a musician? Silly question, surely: a musician is someone who plays a musical instrument or sings. **What, though, is a musical instrument?** Again, to most people the answer probably seems obvious: violins, trumpets, pianos and so on; everyone knows that these are musical instruments, don't they?

At a certain point last century (1931, to be precise), the electric guitar appeared on the scene. It didn't take as long for a beginner musician to make exciting sounds on the electric guitar, but in the end a lot of rock guitarists showed that, with plenty of practice, you can demonstrate advanced skills. It took over fifty years before you could take rock guitar grades, but in the end music education opened up to a relatively new instrument.

Are the DJ decks really a musical instrument? Anyone who thinks not ought to have a go at replicating the techniques that are so brilliantly outlined in this book: these are real skills that take work and practice to acquire. DJs are musicians and DJ decks are musical instruments: we need to say that out loud, and often.

The exposure and interest in DJ-ing in education has significantly increased in recent years. Sometimes it takes decades for education to catch up with social change, but it always happens in the end — particularly when you are talking about something as popular (and as demanding) as DJ-ing.

DJ decks are not identical to other musical instruments: the skills of the DJ differ from those of a clarinettist or rock guitarist. Nevertheless, the skills are real and acquiring them develops true musical knowledge. Through learning to control the decks, furthermore, the DJ gains self-confidence, satisfaction and a genuinely creative opportunity to express feelings through music.

There is room in the world for both traditional instruments and this (relatively) new music-making equipment (not to mention the burgeoning category of 'electronic music'). With DJ decks, you can explore music in a practical way: 'Can this go with that?' or 'Can I pull off this mix?' DJs can compose (be that composing a set or planning the detail of a live mix) or improvise (re-mixing on the spot or diverting from a planned set to fit the moment, for example). And listening skills are crucial: the DJ needs a keen pair of ears and a steady pair of hands. Like any musician, the DJ needs to practise, practise, practise; and then enjoy the fruits of their labour.

This brilliant handbook will help you develop your skills, musical understanding and sense of what makes DJ-ing unique, exciting and important as a modern musical skill. Dig in and enjoy.

To the FutureDJ

This book is written primarily for the aspiring student (of any age), who has little or no prior knowledge of DJ-ing. It is also a resource for any DJ looking to brush up on skills, learn new ones or explore new genres. As with all of the contributors to this book, we are professional DJs and music producers, and more recently we have been heavily entrenched in music education. It is our belief that through the principles and practice of DJ-ing students can truly begin to learn music, build self-confidence and, most of all, have fun.

This book has also been written with the educator in mind. We hope that it may serve as a reference for any teacher who is looking to increase student engagement by introducing a contemporary instrument into their classroom, or simply to gain some knowledge of the alchemy of mixing records. The principles, techniques and knowledge contained in this book fall in line with the syllabus criteria of the major UK exam boards that include DJ-ing as part of their higher education music courses.

DJ-ing styles

The term 'DJ-ing' means a great deal of different things to different people. Perceptions, and the DJ-ing techniques, vary hugely between different genres of music, cultures and countries.

In this book we have aimed to provide all the technical foundations for a DJ in any genre, in any culture, in any style. It was written with the view that there is a place for every form of DJ-ing.

Musical taste

This book has been written at a time when technology has made DJ-ing accessible to many people, having removed the challenges that the early pioneers faced. Anyone can DJ, and therefore everyone can sound the same. The heart of being a great DJ is a great music selection; build up an unparalleled collection and develop your own taste in music.

Beat-matching

A lot can be said about the press-play or press-sync culture, but that is not for this book. What is most important is that, as a student of FutureDJs, you learn how to DJ with respect to the origins of the art form, using your ears. In schools, all our students are taught to beat-match by ear with no visual aids. Beat-matching is a challenging skill which is unique to the instrument, with many artistic and technical benefits that we believe every FutureDJ should possess. Once you are proficient, your mixing style is completely up to you.

Technology

Technology changes, trends develop, genres come and go (and come again). Inevitably, new equipment will appear, and with it will come new techniques and ways of manipulating music. But the core principles will remain the same, just as they have over the last 50 years.

Careers

This book provides a starting point for a creative journey of discovery, passion, obsession and knowledge. It does not suggest ways of 'making it' in the industry. It is written with the view that to truly DJ is to DJ for your true self, and it doesn't matter if that is alone, with one person or with 10,000.

'I think in terms of electronic music, a lot of it will disappear. The machine, the drum machine for instance, will disappear, because computers will eventually disappear. They'll be helping us, but the physical computer will disappear.'

Jeff Mills
fabric: In Depth

Perceptions

Learning to DJ will not necessarily teach you about Western classical notation or the history of Western classical music. It has its own history and unique skills. But can it teach you to listen acutely and critically, to improvise, to compose, to perform and to be a musician? Absolutely. As a DJ, in even the most basic mix, we listen to the two tracks individually, and assess how they would sound when blended together; then we compose: we imagine how we can affect each track to achieve our desired effect. Finally, we turn the dream into reality and perform the mix aloud, listening to both tracks simultaneously, continually adjusting the sounds as we hear them. This requires an extremely high aural awareness, creativity and an innate understanding of rhythm and pulse.

Bear in mind the thought process that has gone into selecting those two tracks. It requires knowledge of harmony; of rhythmic patterns, of the spectrum of sound, of the genre, the artists and instruments involved. It requires imagination. Above all, it requires a perception of musical emotion — an understanding of the emotional and physical energy created by music and the effect it will have on an audience.

A DJ must take into account their audience, their venue, their location, the acts performing before and after them, and consider what they are trying to achieve with their moment behind the decks. The end result is a curated and composed selection of music — an expression of their unique taste, perception and understanding of music. This process will inspire a love and passion for music that can be taken in any direction — any genre, any instrument, any setting. This is not the current perception of DJ-ing but it is the belief of every FutureDJ.

Enjoy the journey.
Austen and Scott Smart

How to use this book

What you need

There is a multitude of equipment available to a DJ. New technologies are developing all the time, making DJ-ing more affordable and ever-increasing the functionality. For the purposes of this book, we have focused on the following three set-ups:

Vinyl turntables + Mixer
CDJs + Mixer
Controller + Software

There are many variations of these — different brands distinguish their hardware in subtle ways — but equivalent functions can be found on whichever set-up you decide to use, however cheap or expensive. Do not let your medium be the reason not to start your journey. In order to learn the whole spectrum of techniques covered in this book, you will need:
— **two jog wheels or platters**
— **a two-channel mixer**
— **speakers**
— **a pair of headphones.**

Audio 🎧

Accompanying audio can be downloaded from **futuredjs.org/book**. Once you have downloaded the music, import the folder into the DJ software of your choice.

If you have a vinyl-only set-up, it is important that you have a number of records of the same style and genre in order to work through this book. An ideal way to practise beat-matching is to have two of the same record.

FutureDJs terms

Tracks	Also known as songs. Throughout the book they will be referred to as tracks.
Deck 1	The left deck.
Deck 2	The right deck.
The platter/jog wheel	We will use 'platter' when referring to vinyl turntables and 'jog wheel' when referring to a digital set-up.
Electronic music	This is an umbrella term for all the genres and styles of music covered in this book.

Key to icons

💡	tips and bright ideas	⇄	sends you to reminders or relevant topics elsewhere in the book
ⓘ	extra information	⚠	warning

FutureDJs

Stage: 1

Warm up

A brief history of DJ-ing (and electronic music)

So how did we get here?

Today you can hear a track on the radio or at a live event, Shazam it, download it or stream it to your computer or phone and use it in a DJ set alongside live sequencing. But surely it wasn't always like this? Let's 'rewind' and take a moment to understand how we got here.

DJ-ing was historically centred around vinyl and the radio DJ. Then in Jamaica in the 1960s a culture called 'soundsystem' developed, whereby rival DJs would aim to outdo one another with their sound systems and, most importantly, their record selection.

From there, DJ-ing would go two ways, in line with the development of new musical genres:

Mixing	Soundclash
Transitioning	Scratching
Club DJ-ing	Performance DJ-ing

1970s New York provided many of the moments that would influence the future of both DJ-ing and electronic music, giving birth to whole new cultures that are still influencing music today. Disco, a sound built on funk groove, was thriving. Clubs such as Studio 54, David Mancuso's The Loft and The Sanctuary were attracting cult-like followings. The 12-inch record had been introduced to DJs by the inventor of the remix, Tom Moulton; when his pressing plant ran out of 7-inch records, he discovered the music sounded much louder when cut to a 12-inch. DJs were dictating the records the radio would play and new, electronically produced tracks were being made with continuous and identifiable beats and rhythms. This hive of activity allowed a handful of innovators, producers and DJs to explore and develop their craft.

Kool Herc set wheels in motion with his huge sound systems and now legendary parties at 1520 Sedgwick Avenue in the South Bronx, New York. He also clocked on to playing just the breaks in Disco records (the parts of the track that have no vocals and are normally just rhythms and beats). But it was a DJ called Grandmaster Flash who realised that if he had two versions of the same record he could play one, and when a section came to an end (normally after 8 bars) he could switch over to the other record and start the same break on the other side ('beat-juggling'). Grandmaster Flash spent years mastering this skill, and people began to MC over the top of these repeated breaks. Around this time, Afrika Bambaataa was building a vibe and organising a scene as a way to get the youth off the streets and end gang warfare. Hip-hop was born, circa 1973, and one could argue that modern-day Hip-hop owes this holy trinity a great deal.

DJs such as Nicky Siano (The Sanctuary), David Mancuso (The Loft) and Larry Levan (Paradise Garage) were segueing (smoothly transitioning) their records so that the dance floor would continually move all night. Francis Grasso, one of the innovative DJs, developed the technique now known as 'beat-matching'. By using a pair of headphones in his set-up he was able to preview a record on one turntable whilst the other played on a second turntable, and by getting the turntables to play at the same speed he was able to mix them continuously. Ultimately, this would change club DJ-ing forever.

In Europe, electronic music was bubbling away. Kraftwerk led the charge and New Order followed, drawing inspiration from the New York clubs. One was feeding the other: an ecosystem developed.

At a Chicago club called The Warehouse, Frankie Knuckles (aka 'The Godfather of House') was at the helm, mixing together New Wave, European synth pop, Disco and Funk. He would play and make edits that no one had ever heard before, and people would ask record shops for the music 'heard at Warehouse'; this was eventually shortened to 'House'. A sound had been established that was clearly based on Disco, but had stronger syncopated beats, more loops, heavier basslines and electronic samples. Clubs like The Warehouse and The Paradise Garage (New York) did two things with this ever-evolving music: they played it continuously all night, and welcomed anybody inside, regardless of sexual orientation, colour or gender.

A similar thing was happening around the same time in Detroit, at a club called The Institute, with a sound now known as Techno. This was initiated by Juan Atkins, Kevin Saunderson and Derrick May — aka 'The Belleville Three'. Led by Atkins, a less funky, more futuristic sound was developing. The blueprint was being laid for artists such as Robert Hood, Richie Hawtin, Carl Craig, Jeff Mills and so many more who would inspire the Berlin Techno sound.

Over the next decades, this music naturally evolved. Super-clubs were built in Ibiza, and people became more creative and experimented with new technologies. There was an ecosystem of inspiration. This was a truly exciting time for electronic music, thanks largely to innovative producers and drum machines such as the Roland TR-808 (a drum machine used in most modern-day Trap tracks).

In the UK, new genres were spawned such as Jungle and Drum and Bass — an entire scene essentially born from one six-second moment in a track on the B-side of a record from 1969 called 'Amen Brother' by The Winstons (now known as the Amen break). Dubstep appeared in the late 90s in Croydon, London, with its roots in Drum and Bass, Techno and Garage music. Artists like Artwork, Skream and Benga became synonymous with the scene.

Elsewhere in London a similar thing was happening with the Grime movement: a sound developed from Hip-hop. Dizzee Rascal is often attributed as the pioneer, with his breakthrough album 'Boy In Da Corner'. And again, like in so much of the music history briefly discussed here, new genres were born from old ones. The second wave of Grime became more polished and made its way into the charts, and so a new, harder, more underground sound emerged called Drill. Based on its Chicago cousin, Drill artists today go straight to YouTube and Soundcloud and have 18 million+ hits on their tracks.

During this time DJ-ing evolved from vinyl to CD and eventually to laptops and digital. Furthermore, the equipment used to DJ would become more blurred. But if there is one thing we have learnt from the history of DJ-ing, it is that change is good and change is inevitable.

Back to the current day

All of the great DJs have certain traits in common: their love for music, their unique taste and selection. Ultimately it is not about the money or the fame, but about turning nothing into something, bringing new music into the world and selecting the right records at precisely the right time (well, at least according to the DJ).

'For me it's very important to mix genres during my sets. I don't like to follow a straight line and to stick to one genre only — I try to surprise the crowd with a good mixture and, when I can, I play some old school rave tracks in the middle of the set, or maybe some EBM.'

Regal

Core values of a FutureDJ

Reading this book will not magically turn you into a superstar or even a competent DJ. To get there you will need to develop the following qualities. Do not underestimate their importance; being a DJ is not just about the music you play, but the person you are. Whenever you struggle, come back to this page and remind yourself of these core values:

Versatility
DJs can find themselves in all sorts of different environments. You need to be ready for any venue or event, whether it is a party, gathering, club, festival, arena or bedroom.

Knowledge
Knowledge of all genres, techniques and DJ-ing cultures will make you value and appreciate all the music you hear in a whole new way. You'll understand why tracks sound the way they do, why people dance the way they do, why songs are structured the way they are, and why people enjoy the music they do.

Modesty/humility
Every DJ experiences successes and failures. The only journey that truly matters is your own. Aspire to be the best you can be at what you are doing. Do not worry about comparing your best with that of others.

Inner confidence
Inner confidence allows a DJ to shine when on the decks; to trust their instinct and to make the right decisions in the moment. Belief in your versatility, knowledge and practice will get you through any situation. It is important to not mistake confidence for arrogance.

Health
Always put your mind and your body first. Look after your ears. Learn to read your own personal level meter and treat your body like you will treat your music — if you find yourself in the red, turn it down.

Perseverance
Do not be put off by your failures. Failure leads to learning, and learning leads to success.

Practice
It is said that to be great at anything you need to practise for at least 10,000 hours. No matter how good you get (even early on), never stop practising.

Responsibility
At its most basic level, a DJ is responsible for the music. For a FutureDJ that is the biggest responsibility of all. Remember the responsibility to your audience, to yourself, to your equipment, and to the environment you are in.

'Find your own magic and where you fit into the musical landscape — anyone can learn to play records and be technically good, but having a perfect sense of timing and a connection to what's happening on the dancefloor will make you stand out. Make sure you practise and practise and then practise some more. Take up any opportunities there are to DJ outside of the bedroom. You need to get out there — whether it be a wedding, a house party or a local bar/club. It will help you to learn your skill, play in different situations and set-ups and, most of all, how to interact with an audience. You will work out what sort of DJ you are going to become and it will make you visible to promoters out scouting — you never know who is in the audience.'

Judy Griffiths
fabric

Types of DJ

As DJ-ing developed in different countries and cultures, it served a range of purposes and was regarded in a variety of ways. Every ecosystem has different expectations of their DJ. Here are a few:

Event DJ

An event DJ is a business person: able to organise themselves, transport themselves and their equipment, perform to a brief and provide a service. Events may include weddings, corporate occasions, and product launches. They must be flexible, amiable and reliable. Their collection must be extensive and eclectic, covering many genres, tastes and generations.
Core value: **Versatility**

Resident DJ

The resident DJ has a regular slot in a venue. It may be weekly, fortnightly or monthly but it will be at a consistent time. Their job is to fit seamlessly with the sound and culture of the event. A resident DJ will feel completely at home in that sound. Little deviation is allowed; these are competitive spots, and there's always someone else willing to fit the brief. They tend to play in clubs and bars in the area where they live.
Core value: **Responsibilty**

Guest DJ

A guest DJ is asked to play for their particular sound. They may cross many genres or specialise in a niche sub-genre known only to a few. They have the freedom to express themselves as they see fit and to do what they want with their time on the decks. That said, they have a responsibility to the audience that turned up to hear them play. They can request the equipment they would like to play on in the venue, whether in a club, festival or radio show.
Core values: **Modesty/humility and inner confidence**

Performance DJ

A performance DJ is a turntablist, a grandmaster of the decks, able to dismantle rhythms and melodies and rebuild them to their own specifications. They compete against each other in tournaments, like the DMC World Championships and Red Bull 3Style. They break boundaries, both musical and technological, searching for new sounds and techniques to push forward their craft. Their profession is online and offline, regional, national and international. They use specially designed equipment for scratching and beat-juggling.
Core values: **Practice and perseverance**

DJ/producer

A DJ/producer is also likely to be a guest DJ. They perform their own music, sometimes exclusively, and sometimes in combination with tracks made by others. They may also perform 'live' sets, where they utilise software like Ableton Live in combination with hardware like drum machines, synthesisers and samplers to compose and improvise music on the fly.
Core values: **Knowledge and preparation**

FutureDJ

A FutureDJ is versatile and knowledgeable. They have the knowledge and understanding to be any type of DJ or musician they want. They have respect for all types of DJ-ing and genres of music. They DJ for the music and for the thrill of expressing themselves through music. They dedicate themselves to their craft and push the boundaries of the art as well as their own. They are the DJs of the future, the pioneers of new genres, new sounds and new attitudes.

'Follow your heart and passion, be patient, make friends, go out — don't stay in. Be more social than social media — or at least do both.'

Severino

'A career in music starts in your mind and will go as far as you believe you can go. So believing in yourself above anything else is the key to a successful career.'

Bec

Looking after your hearing

It's worth taking a moment to reflect on your experience of sound, and particularly music, and how important that is to you. Being a FutureDJ means being able to DJ well into the future. In order to do that, protection of your ears must be at the forefront of your mind from the outset. There is nothing more debilitating for a musician than hearing-loss, and a constant buzzing or ringing in the ears, known as tinnitus, can severely affect mental health. These dangers can be subverted by taking a number of simple measures:

1. **Always wear earplugs in any concert/gig/club environment.**
2. **Take regular breaks away from the music.**
3. **Always be aware of where you are in relation to the sound sources in the room. Never stand next to speakers.**

We interviewed Jono Heale, Director at world–leading hearing protection company, ACS Custom, to find out more. Jono has over 30 years of working 'both sides of the curtain' in the entertainment industry. In his late 30s he discovered he had chronic tinnitus and Music Induced Hearing Loss caused by exposure to loud music.

How do you feel about hearing loss in the music industry?
It's no joke. Tours, sessions, studio, clubs, pubs, even BBC Radio and TV: but no one told me I could be damaging my hearing, which I feel quite angry about really. Loud music over long periods of time will damage your hearing. Fact.

How does your tinnitus affect you?
The tinnitus is a perceived ringing in my ears and seems to sound like two tones at about 4kHz and 8kHz... all the time. This is interesting, as my hearing test showed that the main damage and hearing loss is at 4kHz frequency, which is very common with noise damage. My tinnitus is more of a problem at night, especially when I'm tired or a bit stressed, or if I wake up in the night — and beeeeeep. It's there straightaway and I can't get back to sleep.

What about hearing loss itself?
The hearing loss is more of a problem in social situations, as I can't hear consonant sounds so well, like F, Th, K and S, which usually sit in the Music Induced Hearing Loss bandwidth. I'm now looking into getting a hearing aid.

How loud does music need to be to damage your hearing?
The first thing DJs need to be aware of is that sound is measured in decibels (dB), which is a logarithmic scale. So, every 3dB increase in volume is twice as loud. If it's twice as loud, you should half your exposure time: simple. Here's an example: at 85dB, your safe exposure time is approximately eight hours. At 88dB it's four hours, etc. Now, in clubs and concerts the sound level can be at least 100dB, which gives you approximately 15 minutes of safe exposure before you start to damage the sensory hair cells in your cochlea.

As a DJ, how can you protect yourself?
If you are a DJ, you are three-and-a-half times more likely to get hearing loss and one-and-a-half times more likely to suffer the effects of tinnitus than the rest of the population. But this is all 100% preventable if you take the right precautions. To still hear the music in high fidelity you need attenuating or filter-type earplugs. There are plenty on the market in both universal and custom-fit designs. If you are serious about sound, your health, your career, want to feel the music and be in the environment, you need the best quality earplugs you can afford. Best by far is to go for custom-moulded. These fit perfectly to your ears, guarantee the attenuation and protection required and there's a range of different filters to suit the environment you are working in. ACS Custom has the best hearing protection on the market. The earplugs are made from soft medical-grade silicone, which makes them incredibly comfortable to wear over long periods of time.

Where and how to get your music

Your own personal collection is the bedrock of the art form. Where do you get hold of it? Where do you start?

Whether you have a preference for a genre or are starting from scratch, turn to the genre pages at the back of this book and read about each one. Listen to the suggested tracks and see what appeals to you. Make a conscious effort to listen to each genre, especially if you think you won't like it. If you come across a genre or track that you particularly dislike, think hard about why that is. Is it the vocals, the beat, the groove, the timbre or the structure? There's always something that you can appreciate. Try to put the track in context; think about the origins of the track's components; imagine a setting where you may enjoy it more; imagine why other people may like it. Listen to it again, and again. Does it grow on you? Music is subjective. No one genre has more value than another. They have all derived from different places and cultures and have subtly differing priorities and purposes. Think about your own priorities when it comes to music, and why your preferences developed in the way they have.

Places to discover music

It can all start from one track. The web that you create will be completely personal to you. Every track you like gives you a lead into others. From one track, you know:

The genre: knowing the genre will lead you to playlists, charts, more artists, more record labels.

The artist: the artist will instantly lead you to similar sounding tracks, but also record labels and charts.

The record label: exploring the label opens up more artists, charts, releases and tracks.

The release/EP/single: check the other tracks on the release. They may be from the same artist or others. It may be an EP, an album or a compilation.

The DJ charts: charts can come in various forms. There are charts by genre, record label and curated by artists and DJs. Ever wondered what tracks your favourite artist is listening to?

The mixes: mixes are great for discovering music. Whether they're part of a podcast series, a recording of a live set, or self-released, they showcase a DJ's particular sound. If you find a DJ whose sound you like, the odds are you will discover music you like by listening to their mixes. Find mixes on Soundcloud or Mixcloud, and use Shazam or find track listings to discover the name of a track in a mix. Remember, individuality is key; be sure to find your own sound, rather than mimic others.

Places to buy music

Digital: many online stores offer short previews of tracks. This can be a great way to browse and discover — you will know after 30 seconds whether you like a track or not. Try: Beatport / Bandcamp / Traxsource.

Vinyl: a record shop can offer a unique buying and listening environment, with personal service. They will often specialise in particular genres and the selection can represent the taste of the buyer. Walk in, ask for help, put a record on the platter and, with headphones on, listen.

Streaming: streaming services are a great way to effortlessly browse through music. Related artists, curated playlists, charts and radio are all at your fingertips. Try: Spotify / Soundcloud / Tidal / Apple Music.

'The idea of sharing your music collection with people on a large scale is great. It holds a level of responsibility to the people you're sharing it with to play the best music you have at your disposal. We prefer not to plan our sets and both avidly collect and produce music between gigs, so being able to surprise one another with new music in a club environment is an added bonus.'

Dense & Pika

Quality: when watching videos on Youtube, we always search for the highest quality videos possible, in fact, anyone used to watching vlogs would argue that good sound is more important than good video quality. When we are on social media we tend to prefer to look at pictures in the highest quality; pixelated photos just don't cut it. Music is the same, so start to think of it in the same way.

You will come across various file types: MP3 (128kbps–320kbps) / WAVs / AIFFs / Flac.

Think about music quality like you understand image quality. A low-quality file will produce a low-quality result.

'When selecting music to play it's important to make sure it's music that means something to you, regardless of whether it's popular. This way, you create a musical fingerprint that's unique to you. Don't restrict yourself by the style of music you play, if you like it and think you can make it work in a set, try it. No one will stand out by playing it safe.'

Audiojack

FutureDJs	Stage: 2
Set up	

Components of electronic music

Whether it's software on a computer, laptop or tablet, or hardware instruments, there are a few popular tools for creating electronic music. A good DJ can split a track into its constituent parts and then piece it back together again in their mind. It is vital you know what electronic music is made of, before you start to mix and manipulate it. You will find audio examples of each instrument in the FutureDJs music folder 'Components of electronic music'.

 Components of electronic music

Electronic instruments

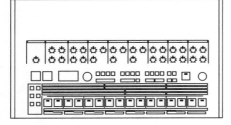

Drum machine
In electronic music, the drum machine is the primary source of rhythm. It is responsible for the beat of a track and is broken down into these percussive instruments:

 The Roland TR-909 is now considered one of the most influential instruments in electronic music history. When it was released in 1983, however, it completely flopped and was discontinued two years later.

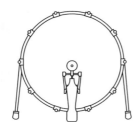

Kick drum
The kick drum is the largest drum in a kit and produces the lowest pitch. It is the source of the thud you hear in your favourite track. An acoustic kick drum is played with a drummer's foot by pressing on a pedal attached to a beater. Electronic kick drums replicate this sound with a very distinct timbre, like the popular Roland TR-808 and TR-909 drum machines.

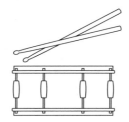

Snare
The snare drum produces a short, snappy sound with its famous rattle, created by metal wires held against the underside of the drum. Typically, it is used in House music on the 2nd and 4th beats of the bar, aka the backbeat.

Clap
Snares and claps are used interchangeably in drum patterns. A clap sounds like two hands clapping.

Hi-hat
A Hi-hat cymbal is operated with a pedal that opens or closes the two cymbals. As such it can produce two fundamental sounds: open and closed. The open sound is a bright, sustained sizzle, while the closed sound is a short, crisp 'Tss'.

 The use of Hi-hats in Trap music is an unmistakable feature of the genre.

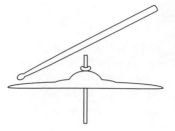

Ride/Crash

These cymbals create a sound with a long sustain. The crash cymbal is used often with a single strike to accent moments like the beginning of a phrase, while the ride cymbal is often played continually to create momentum.

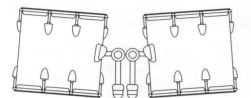

Toms/tom-toms

There are three toms: high, mid and low. They produce a clear, articulate tone with a long or short sustain. They are often used in fills, marking the end of a phrase or section, or in-between the beats, creating syncopation and groove.

Other percussion

Shakers are often used with a sustained rolling rhythm that adds a layer of texture to any groove. Tambourines can articulate a beat with a sharp, high 'tap' but can also fill the high frequencies of a track with a shimmering jingle. The unique, hollow, open sound of the cow bell can cut through a mix and add clarity and precision to any beat.

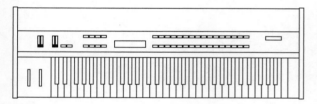

Synthesizer (synths)

A synthesizer is an electronic musical instrument. It produces an analogue or digital waveform that can be added to, distorted, modulated, amplified and filtered to create unique original sounds or imitate acoustic instruments. It is usually played using a keyboard.

 Soft synths are synthesisers that are built into a computer programme, or DAW (Digital Audio Workstation), like Ableton Live.

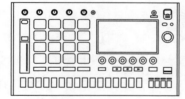

Sampler

A sampler is one of the key components in electronic music and was pivotal for genres like Jungle, which sampled Reggae and Dancehall. A sampler allows you to load pre-recorded sounds and play with them at different pitches or rhythms.

Effects

Effects can be applied to any components to change and 'affect' the sound. You will learn how to add effects to a track as you DJ. It's important to understand that effects are also used in the production of the tracks you are DJ-ing with. Listen out for delay, reverb, flanger, echo and bear in mind that if you can already hear an effect being used in a track, you may not want to add any more.

Other components

Bass
The bass is a DJ's best friend: from sound system culture to EDM, people want to hear bass. There is something primal about it. The bass is the sound that you feel in your gut — it is the BOOM. It can be produced by many components, like the kick drum, pads, synths and toms.

Pads
A synth pad is a sustained chord, note or tone created by a synthesizer. The timbre can vary dramatically, depending on the synthesizer used and the effects applied to it. Its purpose is often to carry background harmony.

Melody
Melodies in electronic music normally give us the hooks, the sounds that everyone remembers.

Vocals
The vocals are any sounds produced by the voice. This might be a rap, a choir, the lead melody or a one-shot sample like 'Fresh'.

'Electronic music wouldn't be so successful without bass. If you think about it, we've really only had amplified bass for around 50 years. Big bass is only a couple of generations old. Before the invention of speakers that could project true bass frequencies, humans only really came across bass in hazardous situations — when thunder struck, for example, or an earthquake shook, or explosions caused by dynamite or gunpowder. That is probably why it is by far the most adrenaline-inducing frequency that we have. Bass gets humans excited.'

Tony Andrews
Founder of Funktion One

Music management

Being a DJ is being a great selector. Start by getting organised.

Your music is your identity as a DJ. You will need to be able to locate the right track at the right time if you are to take your audience in the direction you desire. Discipline and consistency from the outset may save your neck further down the line. A programme like Rekordbox will enable you to access instantly and arrange thousands of tracks using a number of techniques to suit your personal preference. For a vinyl DJ, a box is sufficient. Remember not to overcomplicate this process — the key is consistency, the simpler the better.

Where to save your music

The first decision to make is where your music files are stored.

Media software
A programme like iTunes provides you with a framework, easy access to metadata and offers good integration with DJ-ing software like Rekordbox.

Local files
You can achieve the same organization simply by using the filing system on your computer, but you may miss the playback, metadata and user interface.

Streaming
With a streaming service like Soundcloud, you don't have to worry about storing the files themselves. Beware of being reliant on an internet connection.

DJ software

DJ software enables a DJ to organise their collection and prepare for a performance. Within the software, you can access your music (wherever it is saved) and create new folders and playlists. Your tracks' metadata can be edited and added to, including the title, artist, release, genre, rating, key, bpm, etc. By analysing your tracks, the software can tell you the key, bpm and show you a waveform of each track. You can then add cue points, hot cues, loops and alter beat-grids to make sure your music is reliable and easily accessible.

How to organize your music

Wherever your files are kept, the next step is to create a system that helps you navigate quickly and effectively through your collection. Start with playlist folders.

Playlist folders

Genre
If you are interested in more than one genre or style of music, then set up a folder for each genre.

Event
If you are performing at a number of different venues or events, create a folder for each one.

 History
For the occasions when you lose yourself in an improvisation and forget the order of tracks you played, you can create a playlist from your playing history, even from your USB stick.

'To be a great DJ you have to be a great selector. The records chosen and the order they are played in is crucial to coherent storytelling. The best DJs create musical journeys which reflect their own musical taste and knowledge. The trick is to successfully communicate one's own enthusiasm and understanding of the music. It's all about trusting your instincts and knowing what's in your record collection. Having the tunes is the first step but playing them with character and personality is the only way to truly shine.'

Craig Richards

Playlists

Within each folder come your playlists. A playlist is a list of tracks in a specific order.

Date/session

A quick and easy method of labelling your playlists is by date. If you are looking for a track, you will have a good idea of when you found it. Alternatively, give your playlist a descriptive title such as 'Mix session 1'. You will know the highest number contains your latest tracks.

Energy/position in a mix

If you are preparing for a performance, you could create a playlist for each section of your set, using titles like 'Warm up' and 'Peak', or a simple numbering system from 1 to 5, where 1 is low energy and 5 is high.

Track order

Within your playlists are your tracks. There are a number of ways to order your tracks within a playlist, the choice is yours.

Alphabetical

If you know your track names like the back of your hand or you are likely to receive requests for specific tracks, alphabetical order may be for you. By artist or track name.

Set order

If you have planned your performance from start to end, then put your tracks in the order you intend to play them.

BPM

If your playlist is full of many different genres and styles, ordering by BPM will help group similar genres together.

Key

If your tracks contain vocals or a clear sense of harmony, sorting by key will help you see your options quickly.

Extras

Tags

Use tags to help you group tracks by your own custom criteria: 'Groovy' or 'Dark', for example.

Comments

As your collection grows, adding comments about the structure, components or sound will help remind you of a track.

Rating

All your tracks should be 5-star tracks in your eyes. But the stars could be used to describe the energy or set position of your tracks.

Colour

Colours mean different things, musically, to different people. You can devise your own system to visually denote energy levels, sound, genre or set positions.

How to organize your music

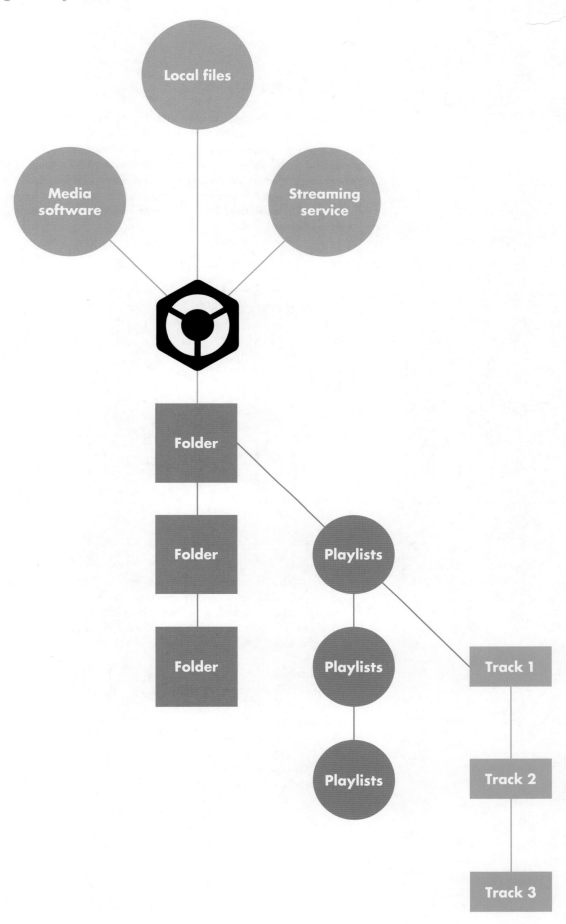

Getting to know your equipment

In the beginning, turntables were the only option for DJs, and vinyl records were the source of music. Regardless of what medium you, as a DJ, choose to play on, you should be able to transfer your skills back to the turntables with a little bit of practice.

Turntables and vinyl

In the 1970s in Disco clubs, DJs like Larry Levan would play 7-inch (18cm) records that would normally last no longer than a couple of minutes. In a rather peculiar turn of events, a remixer called Tom Moulton discovered the 12-inch (30cm) record. When he pressed his record he was quite literally blown away by the sound it created — louder, phatter and perfect for the bass-heavy sound-systems in New York at the time. The 12-inch record was a huge success and allowed artists to make longer tracks, ideal for DJ sets. Turntables are still used to this day because of the feeling they create and the sound they produce.

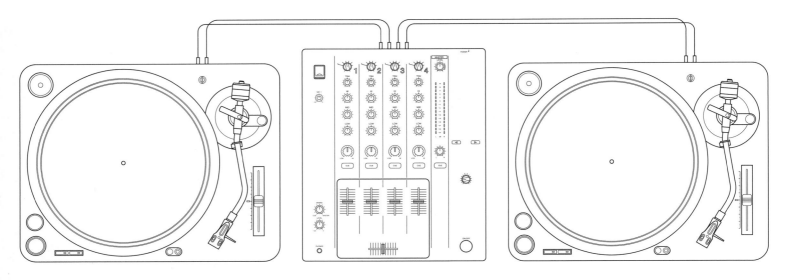

(i) There are three different ways a turntable can be operated: belt, quartz and direct drive.

Advantages
— A vinyl turntable creates an analogue waveform, which can be said to produce a warmer, richer sound quality than digital formats.
— Many tracks are available on vinyl only.
— It gives the DJ a tactile experience — the feeling of physically interacting with the music.

Disadvantages
— Vinyl records are large and heavy.
— They can get scratched and skip.
— Needles are fragile.
— More expensive to buy.
— Lots of tracks are not made on vinyl.
— Turntables need regular servicing.
— Can produce feedback at low frequencies.

Media players (CDJs)

At the turn of the 21st century, Pioneer DJ's iconic CDJ1000MK1 hit the market and was accepted en masse by DJs and clubs alike. Its features develop year on year, but its premise remains the same: it is a digital music player able to manipulate a digital music file, most notably by altering the tempo (speed) of a track. A CDJ can play music from a CD, an SD card or via a device plugged into the USB slot, like a USB stick. The ability to loop, set hot cues, sync and view waveforms has given the DJ new levels of control and endless creative possibilities.

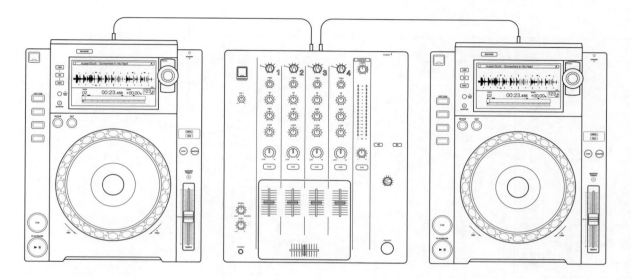

Advantages
— Reliability.
— Visual displays enable you to navigate your collection and view track information and waveforms.
— Playback cannot be easily disrupted by external vibrations.
— Ability to sync with music software like Rekordbox.
— Ability to act as a controller for software (HID mode).
— Can trigger pre-set hot cues and loops and record new ones on the fly.
— Firmware updates.
— The industry-standard piece of equipment: if you can use a CDJ you can play at most venues.

Disadvantages
— USBs can be stolen out of the player.
— Music files can corrupt.
— Files must be in the correct format to make use of all the features.
— CDs can skip.
— Screens can be distracting.

Software + controllers

Many DJs now use software and a controller (which can be a CDJ). Laptops are also used when playing live, using software such as Ableton. In this set-up, the laptop is used as the sound source, and a controller (which could be a CDJ) allows the DJ to control the music coming from the laptop. All-in-one controllers combine the functions of a CDJ and mixer into one unit, creating a more portable set-up. Production software enables a DJ to play music in a whole new way — live in front of people by launching different samples and loops at different times.

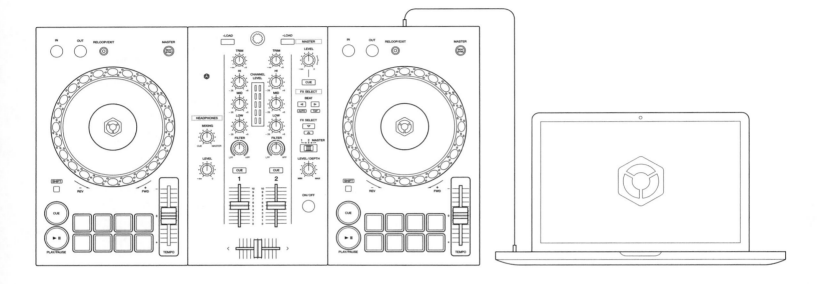

ⓘ All-in-one

All-in-one equipment or DJ controllers effectively have the functionality of CDJs and the mixer integrated into one unit, so no connections between the two are needed. Outputs and other inputs are still available, though the options may be more limited than on a stand-alone mixer, like the Pioneer DJ DJM series.

Digital Vinyl Systems (DVS) You can also use various software to control timecoded vinyl. This gives you the feeling of playing on vinyl, but you will access the music through your laptop.

Advantages
— Music is already on the computer and easily searchable.
— Software can have multi-uses and can be used for live performance, production and music management.
— Small and easily portable.
— Music can be purchased when required.
— Performances can be recorded and broadcast.
— Access to streaming services.

Disadvantages
— Can be unreliable and crash.
— Requires an external soundcard, if not inbuilt into the controller.

Speakers

Whichever DJ-ing equipment you are using, you will need to connect it to speakers. Speakers come in various shapes and sizes. For DJ-ing, make sure you have two separate left and right speakers, rather than an all-in-one bar or bluetooth speaker. Bluetooth speakers may also cause a slight delay.

Passive and active

A DJ will come across two types of speakers: passive and active. Passive speakers require an amplifier in order to produce sound, whereas active speakers power themselves, so they can be plugged directly into a mixer.

Headphones

The number one reason we use headphones is to preview the next track. This is the magic of being a DJ: whilst everyone can hear one track, only you can hear the next track. We do this to:
— Cue up a track or sample.
— Make sure the next track is in sync.
— Make sure the volume of all channels is balanced.
— Check the phrasing is correctly aligned.
— Check you are playing the correct track.
— Compare the components, harmony and groove of each track so you can prepare and plan the mix.

'If someone told you that you could achieve your dreams of becoming a DJ just by practicing every day, would you do it? Practice every day, teach yourself new skills, try out different ways of mixing. Take risks and make yourself stand out from the rest. Most importantly of all, enjoy it and have fun!'

Carly Newman (Carly Carmen)
FutureDJs tutor

'Groove is 90% of the track.'

Dennis Cruz

Signal flow part 1: setting up

It's vitally important not to consider the back of your equipment to be a no-go zone. You must have an understanding of the ins and outs of your DJ-ing equipment so that you can always set yourself up and solve problems if and when they arise.

Signal flow

At the centre of any DJ-ing set-up is a mixer. Connections to and from the mixer can be split into 'inputs' and 'outputs'. Inputs connect sound sources (CDJs, turntables, computers, mics) to the mixer. Outputs connect the mixer to amplifiers, speakers and recording devices.

There are four basic stages to signal flow through your equipment:

1 **Storage device**

2 **Input device**

3 **Mixer**

4 **Output device**

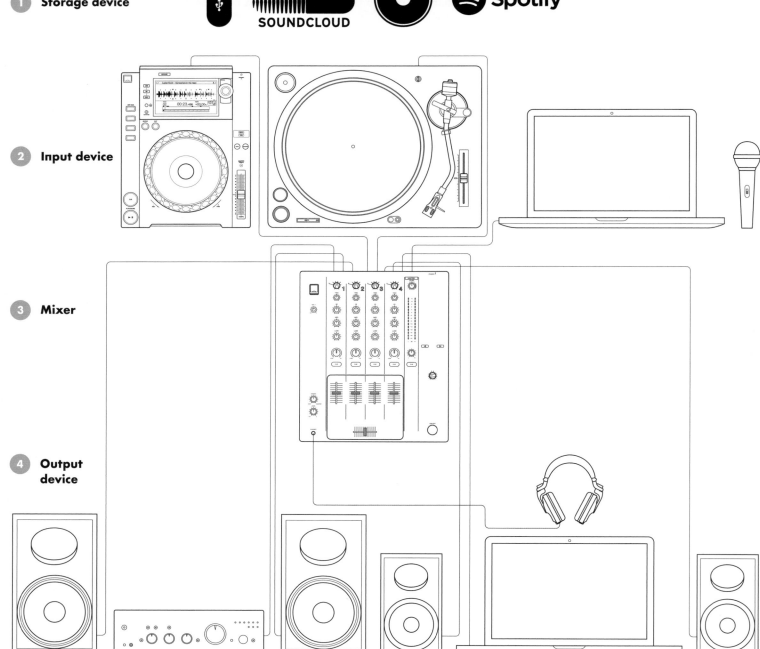

Storage device

It all starts with a storage device. Whichever set-up you have, your music must be stored on a device that your equipment can read.

USB stick/SD card
Good for: Modern CDJs, all-in-one units like the Pioneer DJ XDJ range and laptops (if imported into Rekordbox).
Not good for: Old CDJs, turntables

CDs
Superseded by the USB, the CD is becoming obsolete as a storage device for DJ-ing.
Good for: CDJs
Not good for: Everything else

Vinyl
The oldest and most cumbersome storage device available, yet its analogue technology sets it apart from all current and future devices.
Good for: Turntables
Not good for: Everything else

Laptop/Mobile/Computer
With large hard drive capacities, laptops and mobile devices enable almost limitless storage of your music and access to music production software and streaming services.
Good for: Modern CDJs, software like Rekordbox or Ableton Live, timecode vinyl
Not good for: Most turntables

 Input devices

The mixer does not create signal, it only receives, processes and sends it out. Inputs are the origins of the signal — they are the devices that produce and manipulate your sound. These may include:

Media player (CDJs)
Digital input device originally designed to process CDs, however now more often used with a USB storage device.
Cable: RCA or digital

Turntable
Analogue input device used to play vinyl records. The microscopic bumps and troughs along a groove on the record create vibrations that are converted into sound.
Cable: RCA and earth wire

Software
Software like Rekordbox or Ableton can also be used to send music straight to the mixer.
Cable: USB

Microphone input
A microphone input is unique, though it may not look it. A microphone creates a low level of signal, much lower than other input devices. A mic input is designed to pick up this especially weak signal and boost it.
Cable: XLR/TRS

Instruments
Drum machines, synthesizers and samplers can also be used as input devices. They are often used when a DJ or artist is performing a 'live' set.

 Mixer

The mixer combines and processes the sound from the input devices. We will go into more detail about this later on.

'DJ-ing is very much about the pursuit of the flow state. If it's too easy, make it more challenging, but never chase perfection. Perfection is restrictive, the happy accidents make a set more human.'

Rebekah

4 Output devices

Once the mixer has combined and processed the signal from the sound sources, it is ready to leave the mixer and head for your speakers. The outputs are the pieces of equipment the signal goes to once it has left the mixer. These might include:

Master amplifier/speakers

The master speakers are the speakers that your audience are listening to. They will either be passive speakers via an amplifier or active speakers that power themselves.
Cable: XLR/TRS

Booth speakers

The booth speakers are the speakers you, the DJ, are listening to — the speakers in the 'booth'. They enable you to hear what you are playing without delay.
Cable: XLR/TRS

Recording device

This output sends the signal to a recording device.
Cable: TRS/RCA/3.5mm jack

Headphones

Your headphones are the only output device that can receive whichever single or combination of inputs you want to hear.
Cable: 3.5mm or ¼-inch jack

Cables

Different types of input and output require different types of cable. It's vital to know what these are and why — using the wrong cable, plugging into the wrong input or both — will at the very least create level problems and distortion or, at worst, damage your equipment (or even your ears).

RCA (phono)
An RCA cable is a pair of attached wires with a red and white (sometimes black) plug at either end. The white plug carries the Left signal, the red plug the Right signal. Match the plug colour with the input colour on your mixer for a correct connection. Used to connect input devices to a mixer.

Digital cable (S/PDIF)
A digital plug closely resembles the RCA, however there is only one of them. It is used to connect digital input devices to a mixer.

TRS (¼ and 1/8" jack)
The TRS cable comes in two sizes: ¼" and ⅛". You will find the ⅛" on the end of the cable from your headphones, though you may need a ¼" adaptor to connect it to your mixer. They are also used to connect mixers to output devices.

XLR
The three-pronged XLR cable is the most secure — it clips into the socket to hold it in place. As such it is the most common connector between a mixer and output devices like speakers and amplifiers.

Earth wire
The earth wire comes out of the back of a turntable and is connected to the ground screw on a mixer or amplifier. This wire helps reduce the hums and hisses produced by electrical circuitry that can be picked up by the very sensitive components of the turntable.

ⓘ **Balanced and unbalanced**
Audio cables can carry a balanced or unbalanced signal. In short, unbalanced cables are susceptible to interference. Think of the hum you hear when you place a mobile phone near your speakers. A balanced cable reduces this by carrying a signal wire and an inverted signal wire in the same cable. The speakers output the difference between the two. A pair of XLR or TRS cables are balanced.

Equipment functions part 1

Now we are plugged in, let's take a closer look at your equipment. Across all formats of DJ-ing, the core elements remain the same, so you will soon discover that you can combine them all to suit your style and sound.

Mixer + headphones

No matter what medium you decide on, you will always use a mixer and a pair of headphones.

1 Headphone cue
This CUE button allows you to select the channel you hear in your headphones. Some mixers also have a headphone cue for the master channel, enabling you to hear the whole mix.

2 Headphone level
This adjusts how loud you hear the music in your headphones. It's always best to glance at this before you put the headphones on in case it's up too high.

3 Headphone mix
This adjusts the balance in your headphones between the channels you have selected with the headphone CUE button and the MASTER (the sound coming out of the speakers). You have the option of CUE channels only, MASTER only, or somewhere in between.

4 Trim/gain
Adjusts the overall level of audio signal from the input device that comes into each channel.

5 Channel level meter
Displays the level of audio signal for each channel before passing through the channel faders.

6 Channel faders
Adjusts the level of audio signal output from each channel. Slide the fader cap to the bottom and no signal is let through; to the top and all the signal is allowed through.

7 Master level
Controls the level of audio signal from the master. This is the last control in the chain, affecting the level of signal as it leaves the mixer, on its way to the speaker system.

8 Master level meter
Displays the level of audio signal from the master. If you don't have this meter on your hardware, you'll find it in software like Rekordbox.

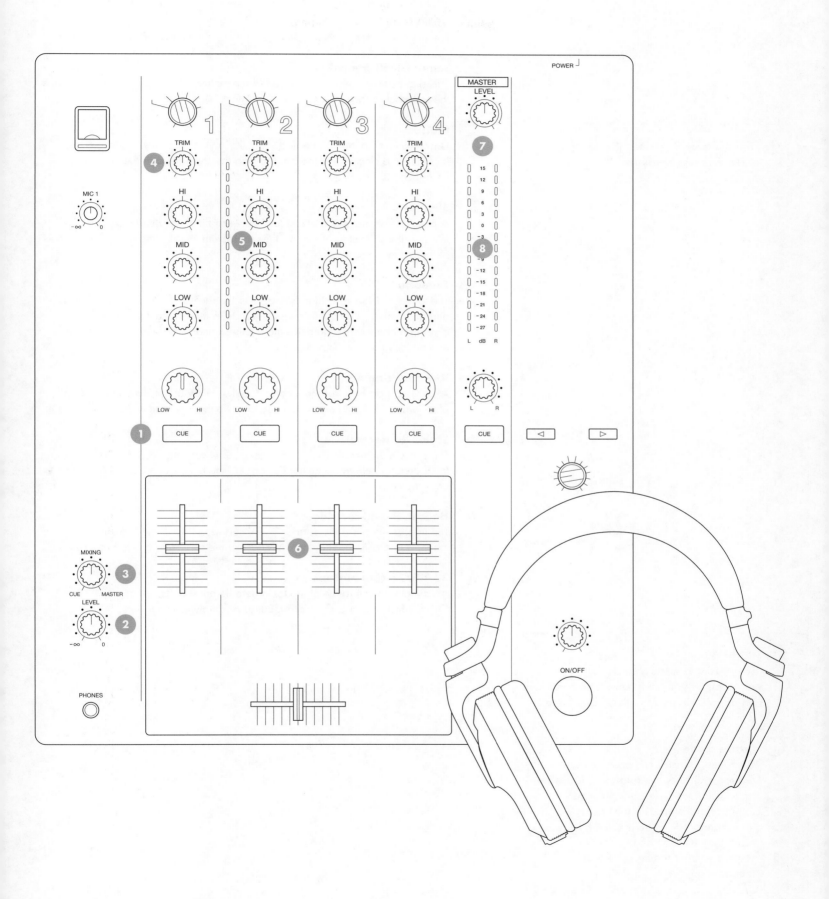

Vinyl turntable

⚠ The platter is a very sensitive component, it requires a gentle touch.

1 START/STOP
Pressing the button starts and stops the rotation of the platter.

2 Tempo/pitch control
This slider adjusts the rotation speed of the platter, which increases or decreases the speed of a track.

3 Platter
Driven by a motor, the platter is the circular plate that a vinyl record sits on. It rotates in a clockwise direction, drawing the stylus through the grooves on a record.

4 Slipmat
A piece of soft material that's placed between the record and the platter. It allows the DJ to stop and move the record without affecting the speed of the platter underneath.

5 Tonearm
The tonearm is the lever that extends over the record. At one end is the stylus and at the other is a counter weight. The stylus must contact the record with a very precise weight: too much may cause damage and distortion, too little and the needle may jump and skip.

6 Arm rest/clamper
A small support base for the tone arm, with a clip that holds the tone arm in place when not being used. Don't try to move the tone arm without unlocking it.

7 Stylus (or needle)
The stylus is the needle-like point of contact between the record and the tonearm. It is extremely sensitive and vibrates against the bumps and troughs in a groove on a record.

8 Headshell and cartridge
The headshell houses the cartridge. The cartridge houses the stylus and the magnets and coils that turn the vibrations of the stylus into an electrical current.

9 33/45/78 rpm buttons
A vinyl platter can rotate at (up to) three different speeds. Check which speed your record requires or simply use your ears.

ⓘ **33 or 45**
Longer single-sided records usually play at 45rpm. If you have more than one track on one side it will most likely be 33rpm.

ⓘ **Battle mode**
Competing scratch DJs position their turntable differently. Rotating a turntable anticlockwise 90 degrees puts the tonearm at the top, furthest away from your hands. This gives a scratch DJ the room they need to beat-juggle and scratch without the fear of knocking the tonearm.

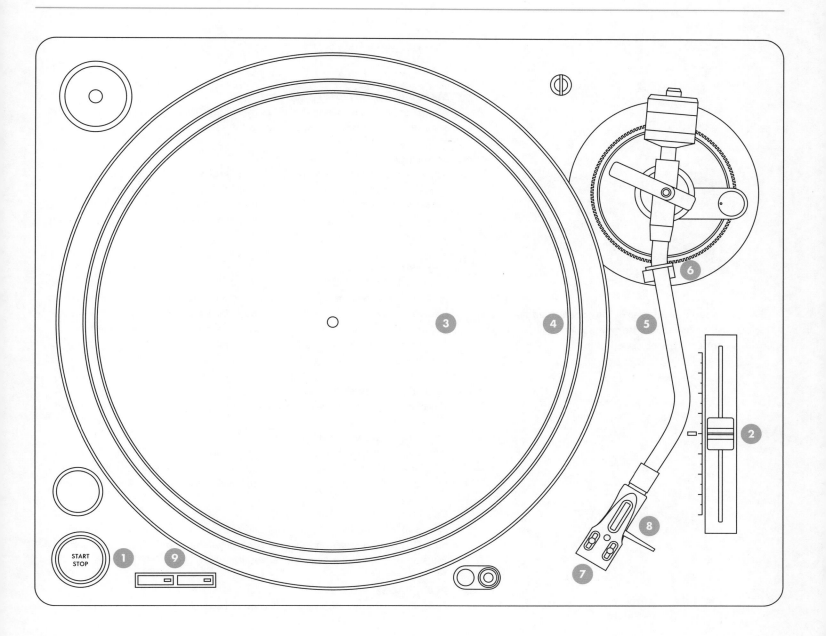

Contact points

The most important consideration is to keep your hand well away from the tonearm. Knocking the tonearm during mixing or scratching will throw you off, sound bad and may damage the needle or vinyl. Because of this most of the contact you make should be in and around the 9 o'clock position.

However, there are other areas that can be used that are particularly helpful when beat-matching. The outer edge of the platter (the knobbly bits, known as strobe dots) can be touched with your finger to slow it down, or pushed around to speed it up. Placing your finger on the centre label, you can brush your finger in the opposite direction to slow it down or, with a little pressure, you can ease it round clockwise to speed it up.

You could try gripping the spindle between your thumb and outside of your first finger and spinning it clockwise to speed it up, or squeezing it to slow it down.

 It can help to keep your finger in touch with the spindle at all times for closer control.

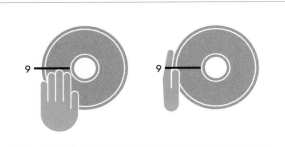

The outer edge is used to alter the speed. Nudging it clockwise or anti clockwise will momentarily increase or decrease the speed of the track.

1 Menu navigator/rotary selector

A circular knob and button that allows you to navigate through your music collection and system menus, and select tracks and options.

2 Jog wheel

Jog wheels give DJs tactile control of the speed and position of a track, much like the platter on a turntable. You can imagine the top surface of the jog wheel to be the record itself and the outer edge (usually knobbly) the platter. As such, touching the top surface will stop the track altogether, just as it would on a turntable.

3 Jog wheel mode

You may have the choice between 'CDJ' or 'vinyl' mode on your digital decks. In vinyl (also known as 'scratch') mode, the jog wheel will behave as described above. In 'CDJ' mode, or with vinyl mode deselected, touching the top surface will not stop playback, the whole jog wheel can be used to affect the speed. This makes scratching impossible but removes the fear of accidentally stopping the track during a mix.

4 Tempo/pitch control

This alters the speed at which the track is played by a percentage of the track bpm.

5 Master tempo/key lock

With master tempo on, the pitch does not change when the tempo control is adjusted. To do this the sound is digitally processed. If you alter the speed too much with master tempo on, the track will distort.

6 CUE

Not to be confused with the headphone cue on the mixer. The CUE button on a CDJ is used to set and jump to cue points. Pressing CUE during playback will stop and return the track to the position of the cue point.

7 PLAY/PAUSE

Press it once to play the track loaded onto the deck. Press it again to pause.

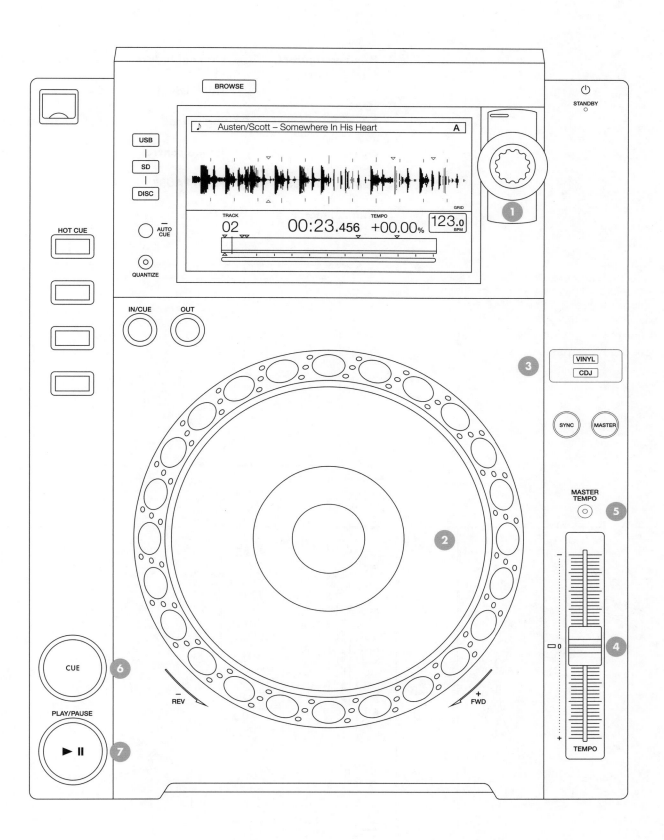

Software (Rekordbox) + controller

1 **Menu navigator/ rotary selector**

2 **LOAD**
Assigns the selected track to the respective decks.

3 **Headphone cue**

4 **Channel meter**

5 **Channel faders**

6 **TRIM/GAIN**

7 **Jog wheel**

8 **Tempo control**

9 **PLAY/PAUSE**

10 **CUE**

11 **Master level**

On the software:

12 **Master level meter**

13 **Master tempo /key lock**

(i) The make and model of your controller will determine which features you find on the controller itself. All the functions above can be found within software like Rekordbox.

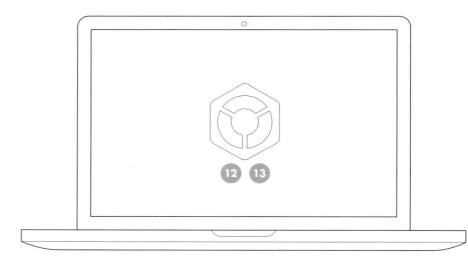

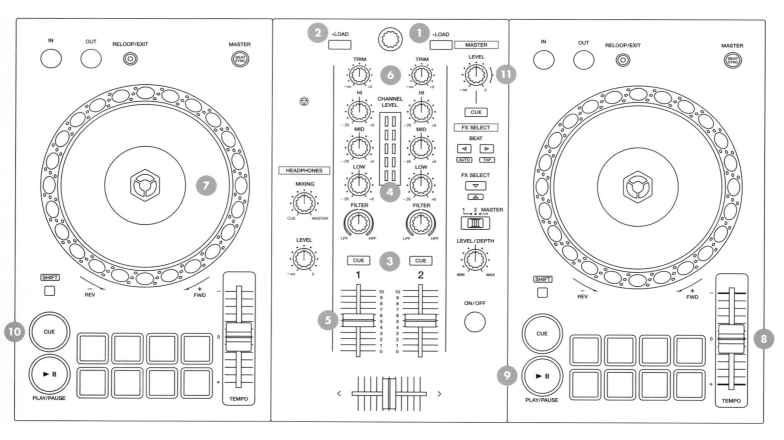

FutureDJs

Stage: 3

Mixing basics

Playing a track

Refer to your owner's manual specific to your equipment if you are unsure, especially if playing vinyl, but the basic principles to playing your first tracks are:

Vinyl	Digital
1. Check your turntables are set up correctly (see 'Setting up/signal flow' and read the manual).	1. Check your equipment is set up correctly (see 'Setting up/signal flow' and read the manual).
2. Place a record on the platter.	2. Select a track using the Menu navigation.
3. Press START/STOP. 	3. Press LOAD to assign the track onto Deck 1. LOAD
4. Unlock the tonearm.	4. Press PLAY on the corresponding deck to start the track.
5. Delicately place the needle on the outer rim of the record, where it is smooth and shiny (there are no grooves). 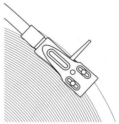	5. On the mixer, push the corresponding channel fader to the top.
6. On the mixer, push the corresponding channel fader to the top.	

 DJs don't tend to use the cue lever! Placing the needle on the record with your fingers is faster and gives you more control.

Play around
With one track playing aloud, start to get used to the weight and feel of the channel fader: practise sliding the fader up and down slowly and smoothly, and then experiment with short, fast movements.

Hearing music in your headphones
On the mixer, press the headphone cue button on the channel playing. This will enable you to hear the track through your headphones as well. Load another track onto Deck 2 and use the headphone cue buttons and the channel faders to hear different combinations through your speakers and headphones.

CUE

Beats, bars, phrases and sections

An electronic music track can be broken down into beats, bars, phrases and sections. Sections are the biggest blocks. The type and combination of sections form a track's structure. Within a section you will find a number of phrases; phrases are made up of bars, and bars contains a number of beats (usually four).

Beats

Music, like living things, has a pulse. You can feel this pulse in all electronic music. When you tap your foot, nod your head or dance to music, you are feeling the pulse. Each individual pulse (tap of your foot or nod of your head) is called a beat. It is the smallest whole unit of music.

Bars

A bar is the basic building block of a track. Think of it like a Lego brick: the studs on top are the beats, and there are almost always four beats in a bar in electronic music. In Western classical music, this is expressed as the time signature $\frac{4}{4}$.

In music notation, you could write this bar like this:

A DJ with a digital set-up sees a bar like this:

Counting beats
Play any track in the FutureDJs music folder and count the beats in groups of four:
1 2 3 4, 1 2 3 4, 1 2 3 4, 1 2 3 4

Counting bars
Play a track from the FutureDJs music folder and, this time, count bars as well as beats:
1 2 3 4, **2** 2 3 4, **3** 2 3 4, **4** 2 3 4

(i) The two numbers in a time signature mean different things. The top number tells you the number of beats in a bar and the bottom number tells you the note value of each beat, e.g. ♪ ♪ ♩

(i)	▶	the triangles shown here represent the beat

Here are four tracks that are not always in $\frac{4}{4}$. Listen and try to work out how many beats they have in a bar:
— Armin van Buuren – This Is What It Feels Like
— OutKast – Hey Ya
— Actress – Lost
— Venetian Snares – Szamár madár
Which classical piece does Szamár madár sample?

▶	indicates the beat
▶	indicates the end of a phrase
▶▶	indicates the end of a section
|	is a barline

4 or 8?
Genres with vocals, song-like structures and shorter track-lengths (around 3 minutes) like Hip-hop, Grime, R&B and commercial music typically have 4-bar phrases. More dance orientated genres like Techno, Trance, and Drum and bass with longer tracks of 5 minutes or more use 8-bar phrasing.

Phrases (aka accents)

Phrases are made up of a number of bars.

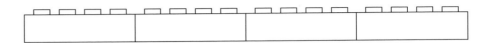

Just as a spoken sentence contains a natural arch, a phrase in music usually starts by introducing something new, developing the idea or posing a question, and then falling to a natural conclusion. It then often repeats. Any of a track's components (the bassline, a vocal or even a groove) can help you determine the number of bars in a phrase. It typically varies between 4 bars and 8 bars.

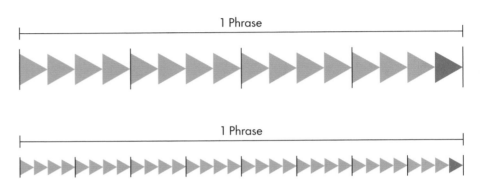

Feeling phrases
Before long, you will instinctively know when a phrase is coming to an end and how many bars are in it. To practise, count the number of bars in a phrase, then restart the bar count with every new phrase and keep track of the phrases in a section in your head.

Sections

A section contains music with the same or similar characteristics. The components — instruments, texture, groove, melodies — remain largely constant, with slight variations only. Some sections are easy to identify, such as a verse or a chorus, but in some genres the difference is much more subtle. The characteristics and the purposes of sections also differ from genre to genre. A section is commonly made up of one or two phrases.

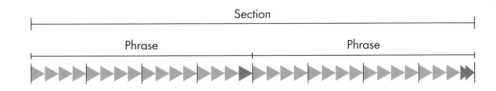

Track structure

For a DJ, understanding track structure is the key to success. On a digital set-up, the waveform can give you an idea of the structure before you have even heard the track. It's important to understand common musical structures so you can anticipate what's coming next. Here is a key showing the most common types of sections you will find in electronic music. Take note of the symbol for each section, they are used throughout the rest of the book.

Yellow symbols indicate some kind of intro or outro section. You will come across a few different types, shown below. Bear in mind some tracks may not have an intro at all and will go straight into the verse or chorus.

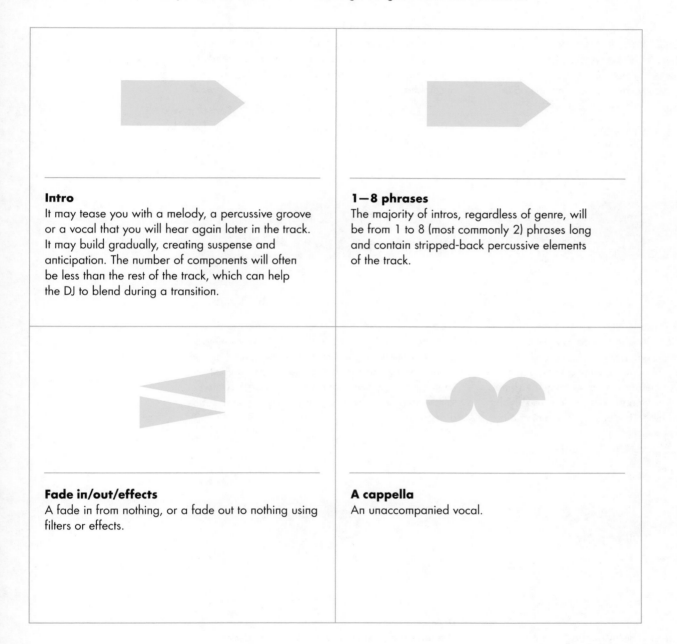

Intro
It may tease you with a melody, a percussive groove or a vocal that you will hear again later in the track. It may build gradually, creating suspense and anticipation. The number of components will often be less than the rest of the track, which can help the DJ to blend during a transition.

1—8 phrases
The majority of intros, regardless of genre, will be from 1 to 8 (most commonly 2) phrases long and contain stripped-back percussive elements of the track.

Fade in/out/effects
A fade in from nothing, or a fade out to nothing using filters or effects.

A cappella
An unaccompanied vocal.

Verse

If there are vocals in a track, it is likely you will hear them for the first time in the first verse. Verses are usually repeated several times throughout a track. Later verses will typically contain the same melodies but different lyrics.

Pre-chorus/Bridge

The section that often appears between a verse and a chorus. It builds momentum and tension and leads the listener towards the chorus with heightened anticipation.

Chorus

This is the climactic section that encapsulates the message of the track. Lyrics and melodies are typically catchy, simple and repetitive, making them easy to remember. The lyrics remain mostly the same each time the section repeats. The music is usually the fullest, loudest and highest in energy, containing all of the track's components.

Hook

The hook is the repeated, catchy rhythmic or melodic idea that often identifies a track — the thing that goes around and around in your head. It can be used interchangeably with 'chorus' to describe a section (although a hook may not have lyrics, it may just be a melody).

Build up

The section that rises in energy, tension and often pitch. It commonly occurs before a drop.

Drop

The drop is a moment in a track with a sudden change of rhythm, bassline or energy. It usually occurs after a break and a build up. This immense release of energy can create a sudden impact on your audience. In instrumental dance music, the drop can be used to describe the section of highest energy in a track, instead of 'chorus'.

Middle 8
An (often) 8-bar section that contrasts more drastically than any other. Where harmony is a factor, a change from major to minor often occurs. Expect a different beat, melody, harmony or lyrics.

Break
Attributed to the birth of Hip-hop, this was originally the section of a Disco track where the lyrics and melody drop out, leaving a percussive beat for the so-called 'break'-dancers to dance over.

Breakdown
Similarly, the breakdown is a section of a track where many features drop out, including, typically, the kick drum. Other components may stop too — there may not even be a beat* in this section — allowing for instrumental solos.

Outro
An outro brings a track to its conclusion. Like an intro, it typically contains fewer components and is altogether less busy. Components may drop out one by one, leaving purely percussive elements. You can expect to find a few variations: 1–8 phrases, a fade out, or even no outro at all.

A, B, C
In certain genres, where melody and lyrics are not involved, it may be more appropriate to label contrasting sections A, B and C or A1, A2 and A3.

 *Here 'beat' refers to the percussive rhythmic material.

Signals

There are several tell-tale signals that a phrase or section is coming to an end, or a new one is beginning. Look out for a small signal at the end of a phrase and bigger signal at the end of the section.

Signals include:
— A variation of a rhythm in the percussion, like the hi-hats or kick drum
— Dropped beats
— Added fills
— Swooshes and uplifters
— Cymbals
— Vocal pick-ups

Waveform 1
Genres/EDM/EDM 3

Listen and follow the waveform and structure beneath. This is a common dance music structure, with 2 breakdowns, 2 build-ups and 2 drops.

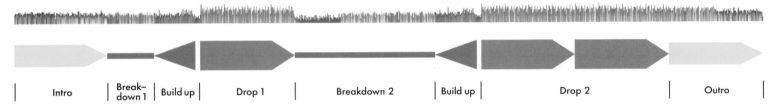

| Intro | Break-down 1 | Build up | Drop 1 | Breakdown 2 | Build up | Drop 2 | Outro |

Waveform 2
Genres/Hip-hop/Hip-hop 4

In Hip-hop, it can be more difficult to see the sections in the waveform. Listen, identify the Hook, then the rest falls into place.

| Intro | Hook | Verse 1 | Hook | Verse 2 | Hook | Middle 8 | Hook | Outro |

Waveform 3
Genres/Techno/Tamas

In some genres, sections change less frequently and less dramatically. Here, the sections gradually increase in energy, there's a break, and then the energy gradually falls back down.

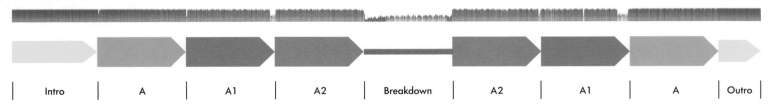

| Intro | A | A1 | A2 | Breakdown | A2 | A1 | A | Outro |

Levels
part 1

All DJ-ing equipment presents you with the necessary controls and meters for you to perform safely within the limitations of your set-up and be the master of your own sound. Without these controls you risk damaging the equipment, your ears and, worse still, your audience's ears.

Electrical current

Sound is carried through your equipment by electrical current. There is a limit to the amount of current that your equipment can process — too much and the current will deteriorate. When deteriorated current reaches its final destination — your speakers — you will hear a broken, distorted version of your music. As a DJ, the provider and controller of the music, you must not let that happen. At the other end of the scale, there is a base level of 'noise' (hums and hisses) created by audio equipment. It's important to keep the signal level as far away from this as possible, yet safely beneath the limits of your equipment.

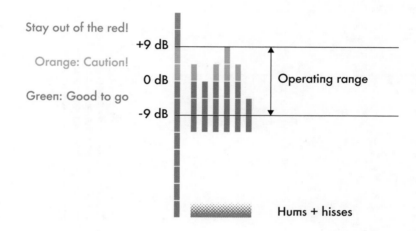

The reality
You will see many DJs live and online go into the red. During your journey you will undoubtedly feel the urge to push the volume louder and louder. Remember to focus on the quality of what you are doing, and the quality of sound your audience is hearing.

Meters
Best practice is to keep all levels averaging around the last green LED on the meter (0db). The coloured bars that dance up and down to the music on your mixer give a DJ a visual indication of the signal volume: these are the meters. The ideal signal volume that is safe from distortion and free from noise is 0dB, or the last green LED on the meter. The aim is for the meter to dance around this point symmetrically — jumping momentarily into the orange but always returning to or falling beneath the last green LED.

Channel-level meters
These are the meters alongside the EQ and trim/gain knobs on each channel. These meters indicate the signal volume after it has passed through these controls. Use this to compare the levels of each track.

The master-level meter
This meter shows you the volume of the signal at the end of its journey through the mixer — having been affected and manipulated by you, the DJ — just as it leaves for your speaker system. Use this to monitor the overall level of your mix.

ⓘ Percussive elements are usually responsible for the biggest spikes on the meter — snares, kick drums and crash cymbals in particular.

Mixing levels

During a mix, a DJ is not only aware of the overall signal levels, they are also constantly using their ears to compare the levels of each individual track: the one playing through the speakers and one playing in their headphones. The mission is to keep your mix at a consistent volume.

Step 1: (III) (Digital only)
Compare the waveforms, the thinner a waveform, the quieter the track.

Step 2:
Listen to the loudest section of the track and adjust the trims so each channel meter is averaging around the last green LED.

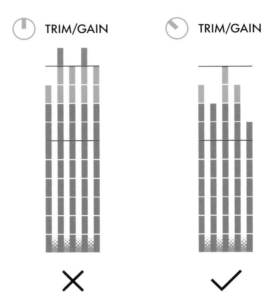

Step 3:
Use your ears. All your meters are displaying correctly, but this does not necessarily mean the volume, as heard by your audience, is the same from track to track. Use your headphones to listen to the cued track and the master together and compare volumes.

Track volume
Not all tracks are created equal
Advances in music production have enabled producers to push the track volume closer and closer to its limit. Older tracks may seem quieter for this reason. A new, heavily compressed track may sound louder than an old analogue track. File formats may also affect the volume — high-quality WAV files will have more power than low-quality MP3s.

Not all equipment behaves the same
Whether you are using a turntable and a CDJ, or a controller and a Roland TR-808, every input device will process signal differently and this may affect the signal level that enters the mixer.

Quality
The higher the quality of your equipment the more consistent the output should be. Your balancing is only as good as the speakers at the end of the signal chain.

'Electronic components can only deal with so much power before they become saturated and produce distortion instead of linear clean sound. If you run into the red, eventually it will melt down and cease to work.'

Tony Andrews
Founder of Funktion One

(i) The loudest part of the track will have the fullest and widest waveform.

(i) It is easy to tell an illegally 'ripped' track from a true high-quality music file: the waveform gives it anyway every time. A 'ripped' track will appear and sound much thinner.

Cues

Cue-ing up is the process of finding the position in the track from which you want to start. Whatever your set-up (vinyl or digital), and whatever you are doing — scratching, blending or playing an a cappella — you will need to go through this process. The CUE button on a mixer will enable you to hear the track in your headphones, so you can audition your track and find your cue without anyone else hearing. On digital DJ-ing set-ups, you can set this point (the cue point) in advance using software like Rekordbox, or as you go. Digital set-ups have a second CUE button, next to the PLAY/PAUSE button, this CUE button will take you straight to the cue point you have set. Press and hold the CUE button to play from this position. As soon as you let go, the track position goes back to the position of your CUE point.

Where to cue-up

Regardless of the equipment you are using, there are a number of things to consider when finding a cue. If you are setting a cue at the beginning of a track, don't presume that you always want to start from where the music begins.

A helpful cue point is:
— on the first beat of a bar
— at the start of a phrase
— a strong and defined beat

An unhelpful cue point is:
— inaccurately placed
— not on the first beat of the bar
— partway through a phrase

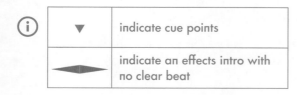

ⓘ

▼	indicate cue points
◆	indicate an effects intro with no clear beat

How to cue up

 Vinyl

⚠ Before doing this, always read the manual and make sure your decks are set-up correctly (for the general principles of a correct set up, see page 28).

💡 If you need to rewind a lot, move your hand into the centre to avoid the tonearm.

⚠ Cueing up should take place in the 9 o'clock position. Be careful to keep away from the tonearm.

💡 Quick movements make the beats easier to hear.

1. Place a record on the platter, press **START** and gently drop the needle on the outer edge — where there are no grooves on the vinyl.

2. Wait until you hear the first beat (which may not be the first sound), and then, with your fingers around the 11 o'clock position, stop the record by applying a small amount of pressure to the surface. Enough pressure to stop the record but not the platter underneath — it should keep spinning beneath the slip mat.

3. Pull the record back, until you have rewound to a point just before the first beat.

4. With your fingers back at 9 o'clock, move your hand forward again to hear the beat of your cue.

5. Repeat this motion, moving your hand back and forth over the beat until you have a clear idea of exactly where it is and you feel in control.

6. Move the record back to a position just before the beat, as close as possible without it sounding.

The record is cued up and ready to play.

Release
To play the record once you have cued up, simply lift your fingers and let the record go. Depending on your turntable, a gentle nudge forward as you release will help the record get running up to speed.

Practise this until you can get the first beat to sound the moment you release.

ⓘ **How to read vinyl grooves**
Smooth black lines tell you there is no audio. You will finds these on the very outer edge and in between tracks. Darker rings show you sections with fewer components and frequencies, like the breakdown.

Settings
There may be a number of
settings available on your
digital decks. These
instructions are designed for
digital decks in 'Vinyl mode'
and with 'Quantise' off. Check
your manual to find out how
to set the mode of each deck.

Alternatively, simply
place your hand on
the surface of the
jog wheel to stop it.

Quick movements make
the 'clicks' easier to hear.

 Digital

On digital set-ups, while it's tempting to rely on the information given to us by
a waveform or an autocue, never trust it fully. The one and only thing a DJ must learn
to trust is their ears, so cover up any screens or digital displays on your equipment.

1. Press **PLAY** on Deck 1 and listen. What do you notice? Think about the components
you hear, and those you don't. Can you feel the pulse in this first phrase? Is the
start of the track a good place for your cue?

2. Keep listening until you hear the ideal beat for the cue. When you hear it,
press **PAUSE**.

3. Place your fingers in the 9 o'clock position on the top of the jog wheel and rewind
to a point just before the cue.

4. With your fingers back at 9 o'clock, move your hand forward again until you hear
the beat. It will sound more like a dull click.

5. Repeat this motion, moving your hand back and forth over the beat, listening
for the click, and making the movement smaller and smaller until you have a clear
idea of exactly where the beat is.

6. Find a position just before the beat, as close as possible without it sounding.

7. Press **CUE**. To test the position of the cue, tap the **CUE** button quickly. If you can
tap the button without hearing the beat, the cue isn't close enough.

Cue-point markers

Cue-point markers can be used like bookmarks. On digital set-ups you can save
multiple cue points throughout a track and they will show up visually on the waveform.

There are a number of reasons why cue-point markers are useful:
— to set the point at which the track starts,
— to mark where something happens in a track (like the beginning
of a particular phrase or section),
— to mark mix in and mix out points,
— to navigate quickly to specific points in a track.

Set all your cue-point markers with the same precision. A poorly set up cue point
can easily throw you off in a live performance.

On vinyl, pieces of tape can be used to remind you of specific points on the record.

Playing
in phrase

Electronic music is made up of sections, phrases, bars and beats. A phrase contains a complete musical idea. It starts, develops, comes to an end and then often repeats. Though they may not know it, audiences are acutely aware of this happening, especially with more melodic or lyrical genres. The cycle of phrases must continue seamlessly as you mix from one track to the next, or you're in danger of breaking the spell. A DJ must pick the perfect moment to start a new track, so that the phrases are in line.

Phrases out of line:

Phrases in line:

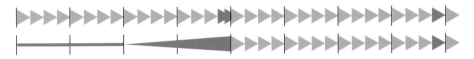

Counting challenge
Count the number of bars in a phrase like this:
1 2 3 4, **2** 2 3 4, **3** 2 3 4, **4** 2 3 4, and so on.

1. Load up a track and listen for the signals at the end of each phrase.
2. Wave a finger in the air, tap your foot or nod your head on the first beat of each phrase.
3. Practise tapping your finger to the beat. Pressing a button is a simple action but it requires a precise and deliberate movement to be accurate.
4. At any point, silence the track by bringing the channel fader down and walk way from the decks. Keep the track playing in your head. The aim is to return to your decks and push the channel fader up just as a new phrase or section begins.

'Every time you hit the decks it's an opportunity to become better. Don't be afraid to make mistakes, because there's nothing more valuable than learning from things that didn't work out as planned.'

Armin van Buuren

Let's get mixing

Load up two tracks of the same genre. The objective is simply to listen to Deck 1, and with Deck 2 in your headphones, press PLAY on Deck 2 in phrase. On vinyl, the process remains the same, but without cue-point markers, a feeling for the phrasing and how well you cue-up will be all the more important.

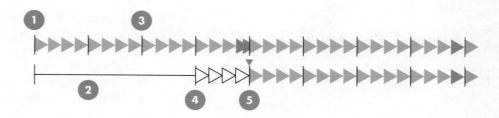

	Deck 1	Deck 2
1	Press **PLAY** on Deck 1 to start your first track through your speakers	
2		Navigate to the first cue point.
3	Listen, feel the beat and hear the phrases.	
4		As the next phrase approaches, tap **CUE** on Deck 2 to the beat.
5		As accurately as possible on the first beat of the new phrase, press **PLAY**.

If it goes Pete Tong (wrong) in your practice
It's fine to make mistakes in your practice – the more you make, the more you can learn. If you miss your phrase, press a wrong button or nudge a slider with your elbow, you may need to stop, hit CUE and start again.

If it goes Pete Tong in your performance
In performance, the pressure is on. There are no second chances, no resets – there is no stopping the music. If you press PLAY out of phrase, your options are:

— Don't panic. The track is in your headphones, your audience doesn't know anything.
— Stop, hit CUE and try again when the next phrase comes around.
— Loop a phrase of Deck 1.

⇄ Check out **Looping** on page 88.

Beat-matching

ⓘ The plural of tempo is tempi.

Beat-matching is the process of listening to two tracks playing at different tempi and adjusting the tempo of one track to match another by ear. It is a key skill in some genres, and not used at all in others. In any style of DJ-ing, where two (or more) tracks are mixed together for any period of time, it is crucial they are all playing at the same speed. On a digital set-up, you can match the bpms on the visual display or simply press the Sync button and you're done — the tempi are the same. So why bother learning to do it by ear?

— **The process of learning to beat-match will develop an instinctive understanding of rhythm and tempi and create a deep connection between you and your music.**
— **You'll be able to play on any set-up – vinyl or old equipment.**
— **You'll be unphased by equipment faults in live situations.**
— **Even if you match the bpms digitally, you'll need to align the tracks. Learning to beat-match makes you a master aligner.**

Being able to beat-match is not essential, but being able to trust your ears is. So regardless of your preferred style of DJ-ing or genre of music, learning to beat-match will develop your understanding of rhythm, enable you to play on any set-up and train you to listen in a whole new way. Once it has become as easy as 1-2-3(-4), you can continue to use the equipment in any way you like.

When two tracks are beat-matched, they are 'in sync'.
To achieve this:
— **Their bars and beats must be aligned.**
— **Their tempi must be exactly the same.**

In and out of sync
The good news is it is very easy to tell when two tracks are out of sync, it sounds like:
— stampeding elephants
— shoes in a tumble drier
— d-dun, d-dun, d-dun

When two tracks are in sync, it sounds and feels like:
— only one track is playing
— the music slots into place
— the stars have aligned

'Visual aids can sometimes throw you off — don't trust them! Instead, close your eyes and listen closely for the element with the most prominent transient. This is usually the kick or snare, other times it may be an off-beat hi-hat or a melodic stab, it varies from track to track. There's no formula but you'll get there with practise.'

Lewis Norton (S9)
FutureDJs tutor

1. Alignment

Alignment is the process of nudging a track forwards or backwards in time to bring the beats and bars of two tracks in line with each other. Whether your tracks are the same tempo or not, this is always the first thing you do after starting a new track.

Tools for the job

Jog wheel/platter   Cue button   Headphones

 + +

Forwards

Here, the tempo is the same but the beats and bars are out of alignment. Track 2 is slightly behind Track 1. Watch out for the feeling that the track is dragging its feet.

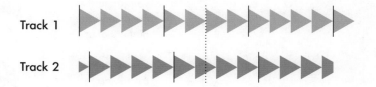

To adjust, nudge Track 2 forwards in time by momentarily increasing its speed. As the tracks are the same tempo, once they are aligned, they are beat-matched.

Vinyl		Digital	
Method 1: Gently stroke the outer edge of the platter clockwise.		Nudge the outer rim of the jog wheel clockwise.	
Method 2: Place your finger on the centre label and gently push the record around faster.			
Method 3: Spin the centre spindle faster than the record is playing.			

Backwards

Here, Track 2 is in front of Track 1. Listen out for the feeling that Track 2 in your headphones is running away from you.

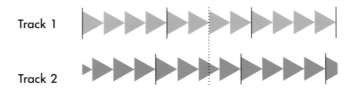

Track 1

Track 2

To adjust, move Track 2 backwards in time by momentarily decreasing its speed on the jog wheel or platter.

Vinyl		Digital	
Apply a little pressure with your finger on the outer edge of the platter.		Nudge the outer rim of the jog wheel anti clockwise.	
Gently stroke the record in the opposite direction.			

Which direction?

In time you will instinctively know whether a deck requires a forwards or backwards adjustment. Initially, this may require some trial and error. If you adjust one way and the alignment gets worse, try the other way. Latch onto a specific percussive component in both tracks, like the kick drum, hi-hats or snare drum, and listen to which you hear first – the snare drum in your headphones or the snare drum through the speakers?

Practice

Using tracks or records of the same genre in the FutureDJs folder, cover up any tempo indications, play one track through your speakers and one track in your headphones and practise adjusting the alignment using the jog wheel or platter.

— Leave the jog wheel or platter on Deck 1 alone, adjust only one deck at a time — the deck you are introducing into the mix.
— Experiment with moving the jog wheel or platter on Deck 2 in both directions. Keep the movement small, practise nudging in tiny increments and listen to the effect. Then practise bigger movements and compare the difference.
— Switch between channel cues to hear each track in your headphones — a quick switch from one to the other may help you notice the difference.

Deck 1	Deck 2
1. START/PLAY Deck 1	
	2a. Cue up b. Listen to the phrasing c. RELEASE/TRIGGER Deck 2 at the start of any phrase
Repeat 3, 4 and 5 for the remainder of the track on Deck 1	3. Is Deck 2 ahead, behind or aligned?
	4. Adjust the platter/jog wheel to align
	5. Listen and wait

2. Tempo

If the first beats are perfectly aligned, but the tracks are different tempi, the beats will not stay aligned. They will drift further and further apart. If the tempi are close (0.05 bpm apart, for example), it may take a few bars until you hear the drift. If they are very different tempi (5bpm+), this will happen very quickly. Listening to the rate of the drift tells you how much tempo adjustment is required.

Tools for the job

Jog wheel/platter		Cue button		Headphones		Tempo/pitch slider
	+		+		+	

Here, the beats are now aligned, but the tracks are different tempi, so the beats soon fall out of sync. Track 2 is faster than track 1. As track 2 is too fast, we need to decrease the tempo with the Pitch/Tempo control.

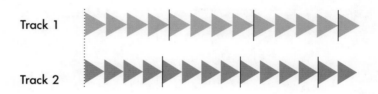

Here, the beats start aligned, but Track 2 is falling behind. Track 2 is slower than Track 1. To adjust Track 2 we need to make an increase in tempo with the Pitch/Tempo control.

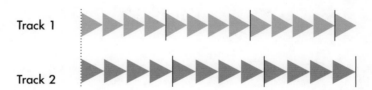

- Really get into the groove of one track — tap your foot or your finger, dance around or sing along. Then switch to the other track and notice how your movement has to change to feel the new beat.
- Consider how often and by how much you have to move the platter/jog wheel to keep each track aligned. The stronger and more frequent the movement, the further apart the tempi are. If only a small, infrequent movement is needed, then you know the tempi are reasonably close.

Pitch/tempo control
Hold the pitch control by placing your fingers on the edges of the slider and putting downward pressure onto the runner. This will give you control over small percentage changes.

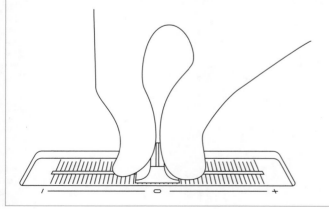

Direction
Increase the tempo by moving the slider down, towards you, decrease the tempo by moving the slider up, away from you. The tempo slider follows the direction of spin of the jog wheel.

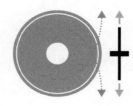

Percentage
The pitch/tempo control affects the tempo by a percentage of the track's bpm. If a track is 120bpm, moving the pitch/tempo control down by 2% will increase the track's tempo by 2.4bpm. The track's new tempo is 122.4bpm.

By how much?

Once two tracks are aligned, the amount of time it takes for them to drift apart tells you how closely matched their tempi are. Ultimately, we never want the tracks to drift apart, so the longer it takes, the closer you are. To begin with, move the slider by 1% (1 notch on the turntable pitch control). The amount of improvement you hear, i.e. the length of time it takes for them to drift apart once more, tells you the extent of your next move.

Practice

Deck 1	Deck 2
1. START/PLAY Deck 1	
	2a. Cue up b. Listen to the phrasing, c. **RELEASE/TRIGGER** Deck 2 at the start of any phrase
	3. Nudge the platter/jog wheel to align
	4. Faster or slower? By how much?
	5. Move the tempo/pitch control slider by 1%
	6. Align
	7. Still faster or slower? By how much?
	8. Move the tempo/pitch control slider by X%

— Try turning off the headphone cue, listening to the speaker for two bars, then switching it back on. This should help you hear the difference.
— Concentrate on the kick drum and ignore all the other sounds.
— Concentrate on the hi-hats, ignore all other sounds.
— Practise, practise, practise.
There is no perfect formula for finding the correct tempo, but with practice, it will click.

FutureDJs

Stage: 4

Moving on

Equipment functions part 2

Here are the new equipment functions you'll need for this stage.

Mixer

1 Channel faders

Think of each fader like a gate. With the handle at the bottom, the gate is closed and no signal can get through. As you gradually push the fader up and open the gate, more and more signal is allowed through, so you hear more and more through your speakers. The trim/gain controls the volume of the signal, the channel faders control how much of it is allowed through to the speakers.

2 Crossfader

Adjusts the level of audio signal output from both channels. As you move the handle towards the centre, one channel increases in volume and the other decreases. In the centre both channels are output equally.

3 EQs

EQ is short for equalisation. The EQs affect the volume of frequencies in each channel. There are normally three frequency ranges: low, mid and high. Turning the knob anticlockwise (from 12 o'clock to 7 o'clock) decreases the volume, while turning clockwise (12 o'clock to 5 o'clock) increases the volume of the frequency range.

4 Input selector

Standalone mixers can be connected to different types of input devices. CDJs, turntables and microphones send audio signal to the mixer of varying degrees of strength. Selecting the channel type allows the mixer to process the type of signal coming from the input device. The standard input types are Line, Phono and Digital.

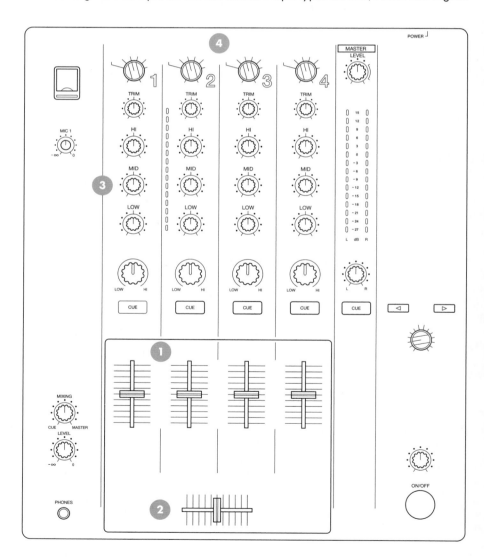

(i) A rotary mixer uses large knobs rather than faders to control the volume of the channels.

Media player (CDJ)

 Hot cues/performance pads

A hot cue is a point in a track that can be instantly jumped to at the touch of a button, enabling a DJ to restructure a track according to the needs of their mix.

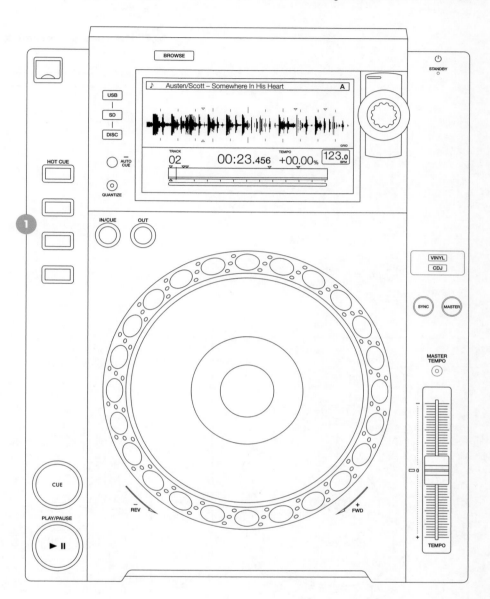

 See **Signal flow part 2**, page 65, for more info.

Laptop + controller

1. **Crossfader**
2. **EQs**
3. **Hot cues/performance pads**

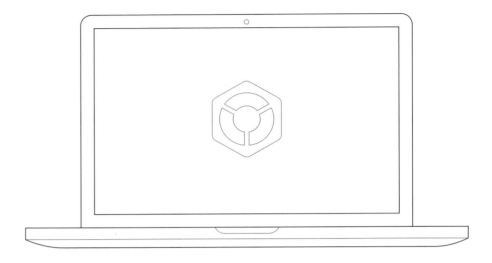

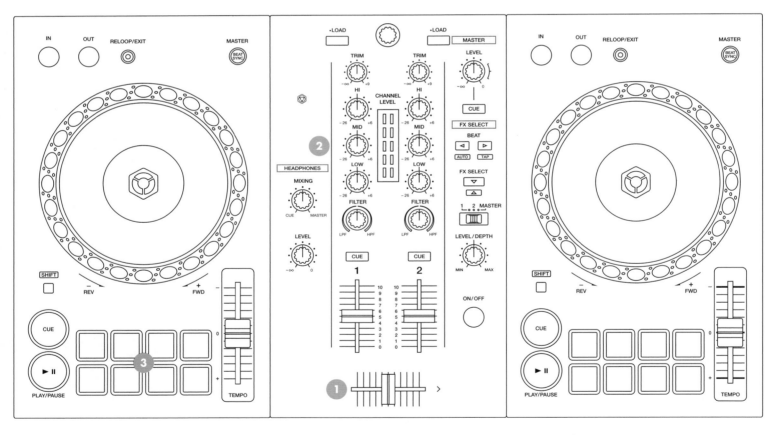

Levels part 2: balancing

When DJs listen to music, they are constantly analysing the sound they are hearing. They are thinking about the components, they are thinking about the structure (the beats, bars, phrases and sections) and they are thinking about the balance of frequencies.

Importantly, DJs do not just think about one track. They compare the balance of frequencies between two or more sound sources. Just as you adjust the levels to make sure the overall volume is the same, a DJ must adjust the EQs, where necessary, to keep the frequency ranges balanced across all sound sources.

Frequency

The frequency of sound determines its pitch. High frequencies produce high pitches, low frequencies produce low pitches. Every note on a piano has a specific frequency; the higher the note the higher the frequency, the lower the note the lower the frequency.

You can visualise all sound by its frequency. Here is an example of a frequency curve of a track. Along the x axis is the frequency (in Hz) and the y axis shows the volume (in dB) of the frequency. We can divide the frequency range into three sections: low, mid and high.

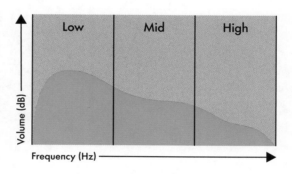

Equalisation (EQs)

The EQs on a mixer take control of these frequency ranges. There are three knobs: low, mid and high.

Each knob controls the volume of its frequency range. In the 12 o'clock position, the signal is not affected at all. Turning the knob clockwise will boost the frequency, increasing its volume, while turning anti clockwise will cut the frequency, reducing its volume.

(i) Some mixers actually have four frequency ranges: low, low-mid, mid and high.

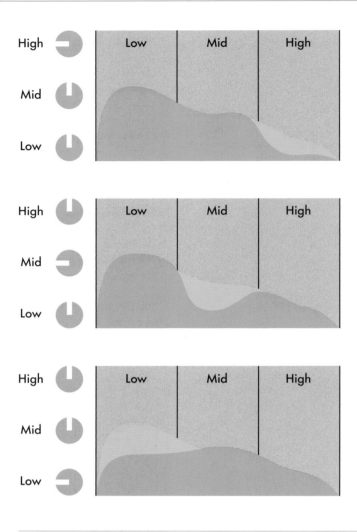

Components

Listen to a track and consider the components below and which frequency range they sit in. Play around with the EQs and listen to each component increase or decrease in volume as you turn the knobs.

High: Crash/Ride, hi-hats, shakers, triangle
Mids: Vocals, synths, pads, snare, clap
Lows: Kick drums, low-toms, basslines

The loudest frequencies in a track tend to be the lows.

⚠ Increasing the volume of a frequency range (especially the low-end) will increase the overall volume of the track. Always check the level meters and stay out of the red.

Balancing during a mix

The frequency distribution of every track is different. One may have particularly loud high-frequency hi-hats and ride cymbals; another may have a strong mid-frequency synthesizer melody, and another may have a soft low-frequency kick-drum. Being aware of this gives a DJ better control over their transitions and the energy of their mix.

Signal flow part 2: the mixer

The mixer is the heart of a DJ set-up. It is the vital connection between the ins and outs, combining all the ins exactly in the way you want and then sending the signal towards the speakers. Each column of knobs, buttons and faders is assigned to one input device. There are usually two or four channels, but once you know one channel, you know them all. If you are twisting knobs and nothing is happening, check you are using the correct channel.

1 Input selector
Line: Used for CDJs, typically connected with an unbalanced RCA cable.

Phono: Used for turntables, also with an unbalanced RCA cable. Though the cable is the same, the input is very different. A record produces a frequency curve with a much stronger high frequency response relative to the low frequencies. The phono input equalises this curve to create a 'flat' signal as it enters the mixer.

Digital: Also used for CDJs or laptops.

2 Trim/gain
Adjusts the level of signal from the input device.

3 EQs
Boosts or cuts frequency ranges as the signal passes through.

4 Channel level meter
Visualises the level of signal after passing through the gain/trim and effects like EQs.

5 CUE
Sends the signal to your headphones.

6 Channel fader
Controls the amount of signal allowed through.

7 Crossfader
If assigned, controls the fade between channels assigned to A and B.

8 Record out
Connects the signal to a recording device.

9 Booth out
Connects the signal to speakers in the DJ booth.

10 Master level meter
Visualises the level of signal before leaving the master out.

11 Master out
Connects the signal to the master speakers.

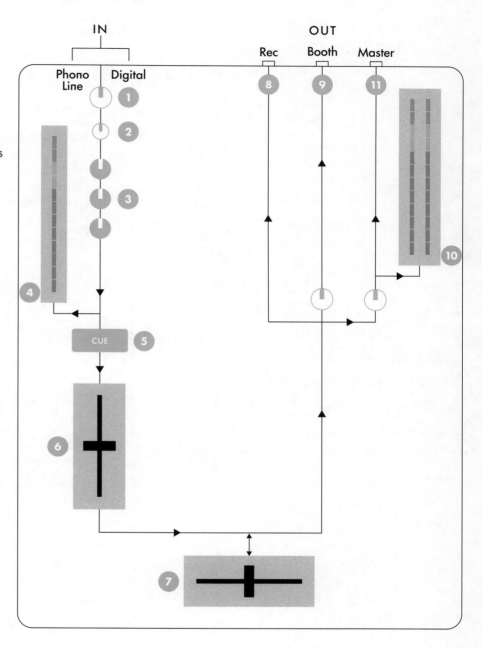

Transitions

Transitioning is the process of changing from one track to another. The way in which you do this can define you as a DJ. It is your opportunity to express yourself creatively and show your technical prowess.

All transition techniques can be loosely fitted into two categories: blend and cut. You can choose to transition smoothly or suddenly, or anywhere in between. The style and genre of the music may limit your options. Some genres favour blends over cuts, and other cuts over blends, but let creativity be your driving force, not the status quo.

Try any of these techniques with the tracks available in the FutureDJs music folder.

 Genres / EDM
/ Disco
/ Drum + Bass
/ Dubstep
/ Garage/2-step
/ Grime
/ Hip-hop
/ House
/ Tech House
/ Techno
/ Trap
/ Trance

'After a while you'll instinctively know which kinds of tracks will fit together, when to push and pull the pitch and which frequencies to swap in order to keep your levels in check.'

James Zabiela

Blends

A blend is a transition between one track and the next, where the two tracks overlap for an amount of time. Blends can be short, long, seamless or sudden. They enable a DJ to create a never-ending stream of music. The kind of blend you use will depend on the structure and components of each track, and the effect you want to achieve.

Tools for the job:

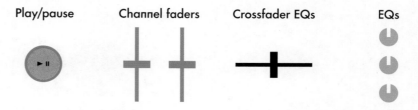

Play/pause   Channel faders   Crossfader EQs   EQs

Basic principles

Fade in, fade out
This is the most basic of them all. Fade in track 2, then fade out track 1.

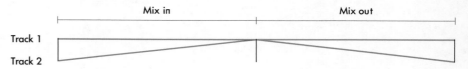

Fade in, mix together, fade out
Fade in track 2, play them together, then fade out track 1.

Fade in, drop out
Fade in track 2, immediately drop out track 1.

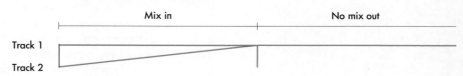

ℹ **Extended blends**
In some genres, like House and Techno, blends can go on for a long time. The combination of two tracks (or more) can seem to become a track itself. This is where a DJ becomes a composer, sculpting their chosen sounds into something entirely new and unique.

⇄ See **Looping** on page 88. Looping can enable a blend to go on for even longer.

Duration
Blends can last from one phrase to eight phrases or more. The genre, structure of your tracks and your personal mixing style will determine how long you blend for and how you do it.

EQs

EQs enable a DJ to carve out space for a new track to slot into, as well as giving them control of the overall level of the mixed signals.

Levels

Playing two tracks at the same time without EQ adjustment can push your levels into the red. The lows are the loudest frequency range of a track in electronic music. Introducing a second bass-heavy track into the mix may push the master level meter into the red.

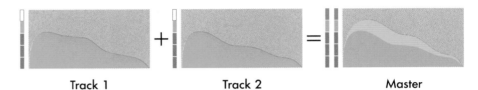

Track 1   Track 2   Master

As we don't want two kick drums kicking at the same time, cut the bass frequency on one track in the mix. This will enable you to play two tracks together.

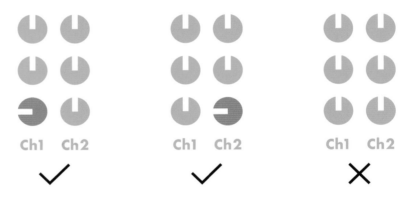

Ch1   Ch2   Ch1   Ch2   Ch1   Ch2

✓   ✓   ✗

Turn down, not up

Be wary of boosting EQs. Tracks are mastered to be as loud and as close to the limits as possible. Boosting the volume further with the EQs can result in distortion. Get into the habit of not adding too much bass without taking some away from the other channel.

The bass swap

One of the best tools any DJ has is the control of the low frequencies – the bass. Take this out and your audience will be yours the moment you bring it back in; just make sure you don't do it too often, because people need bass – it's a primal thing. The bass swap is the moment you transfer the energy from the first track to the second by turning down the bass on Track 1 and, at the same time, turning up the bass on Track 2.

Ch1   Ch2

Mids and highs

The mid and high frequencies do not affect the overall volume as much as the bass. Use them to create space for elements to come through the mix. Tracks combine better when there is space available for a new element to enter into. If Track 1 is taking up this frequency range and you try to introduce another track in the same range, it will be covered, the sound will be muffled, and the mix will sound messy. Use your ears to analyse which ranges are being used more by each track, and then adjust the mids and highs to help the two combine.

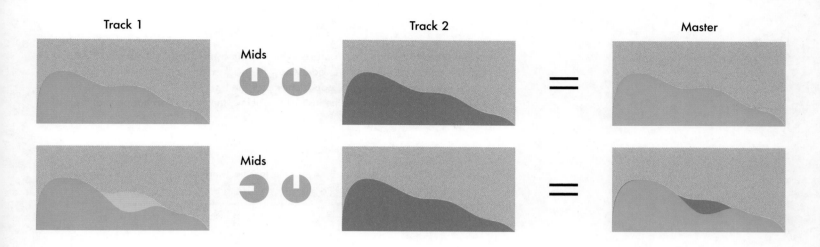

Track 1   Mids   Track 2   =   Master

Remember that the EQs shape the amount of the frequency range you hear, they don't alter the frequencies themselves. If elements of two tracks don't mix well together, turning them down won't entirely fix the problem.

Fade in, fade out

Common in: Hip-hop, Commercial, Grime, House
Here's an example of a fade in–fade out blend that lasts two phrases, with a bass swap at the end of the first phrase.

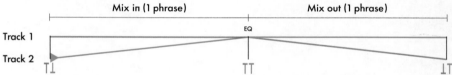

	Deck 1	Deck 2
1	With Track 1 playing...	Find a good cue point at the start of the track and cue up.
2		At the start of a phrase, release Track 2.
3		Align Deck 2 with Deck 1 in your headphones.
4		Turn the bass EQ to 9 o'clock.
5		Push the channel fader up to introduce Deck 2 into the mix.
6	At the end of the phrase, bass swap.	
7	Slowly pull the channel fader towards you until Deck 1 is out of the mix.	

ⓘ ▶ tells you when the track starts

Fade in, mix together, fade out

Try this blend that lasts four phrases, with two phrases in the middle where the tracks play together. Use this time to adjust how the tracks blend together with the mid and high EQs. There are several opportunities for the bass swap, at the end of the first, second or third phrases. In the instructions below, the bass swap happens at the end of the third phrase.

Common in: Techno, Tech-House

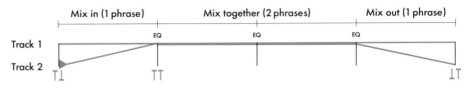

> 'Become familiar with the style of mixing associated with your favourite genre, but don't be afraid to borrow techniques from other styles.'
>
> **Holly Lester**

		Deck 1	Deck 2
1		With Track 1 playing...	Find a good cue point at the start of the track and cue up.
2			At the start of a phrase, release/ trigger Track 2.
3			Align Deck 2 with Deck 1 in your headphones.
4			Cut the bass, mid and high EQs
5			Push the channel fader up to introduce Track 2 into the mix.
6		Gradually swap the mids and highs, listening to the effect all the time.	
7		At the end of the third phrase, swap the bass.	
8		Gradually take Track 1 out of the mix with the channel fader.	

Fade in, drop out

These blends are effective when you want to transition quickly with impact. The whole transition lasts just one phrase. You have got to be quick with your fingers and confident with your feel for phrases. This blend could be done with the channel faders or the crossfader.

Common in: Hip-hop, Commercial, Grime

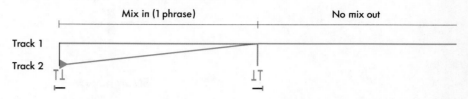

	Deck 1	Deck 2
1	With Track 1 playing...	Find a good cue point at the start of the track and cue up.
2		At the start of a phrase, release/trigger Track 2.
3		Align Deck 2 with Deck 1 in your headphones.
4		Slowly push the channel fader up to introduce Track 2 into the mix.
5	Immediately pull the channel fader (crossfader) shut.	

'Two things I think are important: always follow your own intuition when selecting music and accept that making mistakes is crucial in order to grow.'

Len Faki

Cuts

A cut is a transition where one track is instantly changed to another. As there's no overlap, cuts are helpful when mixing between genres or tempi, or for a sudden change of energy. Timing and a feel for phrasing are everything.

Tools for the job:

The crossfader

Straight cut

The straight cut is quick and simple. Play Track 2 in phrase and use the crossfader to snap quickly from one deck to the other.

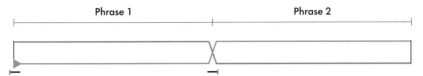

	Deck 1	Deck 2
1	With Track 1 playing...	
2		At the start of a phrase, press play on Deck 2.
3		Align Deck 2 with Deck 1 in your headphones.
4	At the end of the phrase, quickly snap the crossfader from A to B as accurately as possible on the beat.	

Drop in

A 'drop in' literally means you are going to drop the next track straight into the mix and simultaneously cut out the old track using the crossfader. This requires accurate timing and a perfectly cued-up track in your headphones.

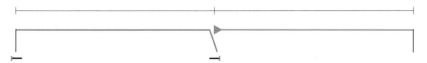

	Deck 1	Deck 2
1	With Track 1 playing...	
2		Cue-up Deck 2 using the jog wheel/ platter in your headphones. Listen for the click and hold the track just before the beat.
3		At the start of the phrase, release/ trigger Track 2 on the beat and at the same time snap across the crossfader from A to B.

Flare

There are a number of techniques a DJ can use to add a little flare to their blends or cuts, or to emphasise and embellish a track while it's playing. Here are a few examples.

Tools for the job:

Jog wheel   Platter

Baby scratch

When you are cueing-up a deck on a platter or jog wheel, the action of moving your hand back and forth over the beat is essentially the same technique required for a baby scratch. With your hand in the 9 o'clock position and your wrist slightly raised so only the tips of your fingers touch the platter/jog wheel, move forwards and backwards. Experiment with the length and speed of your scratch and be rhythmical. Aim for a nice 'chukka-chukka' sound.

Drop in with baby scratch

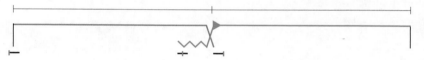

	Deck 1	Deck 2
1	With Track 1 playing...	
2		Cue-up Track 2 using the jog wheel/ platter in your headphones.
3	Move the crossfader to the centre, so both decks can be heard.	
4		As the end of the phrase approaches, move the crossfader into the middle and play with some baby scratches.
5		At the start of the phrase, release/ trigger Track 2 on the beat and at the same time snap across the crossfader from Deck 1 to Deck 2.

 See **Baby scratch** on page 105 for a more in-depth breakdown.

Spinback

Sometimes you will want to exit the track quickly, and at the same time make a point of it. You may even choose to play the track again because the crowd responded so well or because you need to keep the beat going. This is a technique first introduced by the soundclash DJs in Jamaica. During a clash, if a DJ wants to 'flex' their music they can replay it — reload it or mask the transition between two songs.

To perform a spinback, continuously turn the platter/jog wheel at speed in an anti-clockwise direction, or spin it hard with one motion.

Tools for the job:

Jog wheel   Platter

<table>
<tr><td>(i)</td><td>**Reload/wheel up** ⟳</td></tr>
</table>

(i) **Reload/wheel up** ⟳
A reload is a particularly important technique in genres like genres like Grime and Drum and Bass. If a crowd absolutely loves a track, perform a spinback and start the track again.

Drop in with spin back

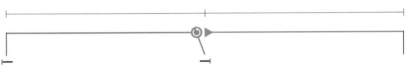

	Deck 1	Deck 2
1	With Track 1 playing...	
2		Cue-up Deck 2 using the jog wheel or platter in your headphones.
3	In the last bar of the phrase, spin back Deck 1.	
4		At the start of the phrase, release/trigger Track 2 on the beat and at the same time snap across the crossfader from A to B.

Beat repeat

As is often the case, the origins of this technique are on the turntables. It is a beat-juggling technique that requires two of the same record. By purposefully playing them slightly out of alignment with each other (usually by a beat, or half a beat) and then cutting from one to the other using the crossfader, the effect of repeating beats can be created. This is called beat-cutting on turntables. On digital equipment this can be replicated at the touch of a button, and with much added flexibility. But remember, being easy doesn't make it effective. Use your knowledge of phrases, your feeling for beats and bars — and remember 'less is more'. 'Slip' mode allows the track to continue from the real-time playback position after the button is released.

Tools for the job:

Performance pads

Where to transition

You are cued up, beat-matched, and you know the types of transition available to you. Where do you start your transition? At what point in the track do you start your blend? Where's the best place for a drop in? There are key principles, but the only real limit is your imagination.

The key is energy. Energy is the amount of lift and momentum that is felt when hearing music. It is subjective and affected by environment, situation, space, mood, atmosphere, and the music that came before. The kind of energy you want in your sound will determine the genres you use, the tracks you use, the way you construct a mix, the way you transition between those tracks and the way you perform.

The energy of a track is never static; there is a flow that closely follows its structure. The better you understand the structure and flow of energy through a track (see below), the better your transitions will be.

During the chorus you can expect the highest levels of energy. If there's a drop, the highest energy will be there. If there are two drops, the second will most likely be greater than the first. If the structure is unclear, a track usually peaks about two-thirds of the way through. During the breakdown you will likely find the lowest, and the intros and outros are somewhere in-between.

 See pages 43 to 45 for a key to these symbols.

Intros and outros contain fewer components and take up fewer frequencies. They have more space in them for new components to be heard over the top, which makes them the obvious choice for your transition.

Track 1

Track 2

To maintain a high level of energy, match up a decrease in energy in Track 1 with an increase in Track 2. This will take the listener's attention, while the decrease in Track 1 will also give more space for Track 2 to be heard:

Track 1

Track 2

This principle can lead you to transition anywhere within a track with a blend or a cut. During your practice, challenge your creativity by transitioning in unorthodox places.

Vocals
If you are mixing tracks with vocals, there are a few considerations.
1. Don't cut a vocal off mid-phrase
2. Don't fade in a vocal slowly
3. Don't play two vocals at the same time

Considerations when choosing a transition

Think about what you are trying to achieve by mixing two tracks together. Do you want to increase, decrease or change the energy? Surprise your audience? Transition to a new track without them knowing? Where does the transition sit within your overall mix, and how does that affect the transition? These thoughts can be broken down into the following categories:

Structure
No matter how technically good your blending or cutting skills may be, if it's out of phrase or in the wrong section, you are unlikely to achieve your desired effect. Knowing your beats, bars, phrases and sections is crucial. Structure will determine what kinds of transitions are available to you.

> **Ask yourself:**
> Where is the climax of the track?
> How does the energy change throughout the track?
> What kind of sections are there? Are there verses and choruses?
> How long are the phrases?
> How much time have you got?

Timbre (components and frequencies)
Always consider the components present in both tracks at the points you want to transition. Blending similar components into one another may be difficult, but tracks that are very dissimilar may not combine well either. The key is space. For a track to combine well with another, it needs space in order to be heard.

> **Ask yourself:**
> Are there vocals?
> What components and frequencies are dominating each track?
> Will they blend well together?

See **Where to transition** on page 75.

Energy

Every track has a unique energy that imprints a particular feeling on the listener, whether subtle or obvious. In a transition the energy is transferred from one track to another. A DJ can do this sensitively, letting the unique energies of the tracks speak for themselves; they can enhance or manipulate the energy of a track and change how it's heard; or they can create an entirely new energy.

> Ask yourself:
> How does the energy change throughout each track?
> Where is the lowest point of energy?
> How would you describe the energy?
> How does the energy change from track 1 to track 2?

Harmony

If a track contains any vocals, melody, piano/guitar/acoustic instruments or moving basslines, you can be confident it contains a significant amount of harmonic material and so is in a particular key. It is important to consider which key each track is in and understand the effect this has. If the keys do not relate well, you may want to consider transitioning between less harmonic, more percussive areas of the tracks, or you may decide a shorter transition, like a cut, is the best option.

See **Harmonic mixing** on page 78 for more information on how keys relate.

Tempo

A DJ can change the tempo to match another track. Change it too much, however, and it will distort and lose its impact.

The overall mix shape

Remember to consider the overall shape of your mix, whether it's three tracks long or 40, and how each transition contributes to that shape.

(i) A DJ is not confined by the structure of the tracks in front of them, but has many tools at their disposal that enable them to change the energy level of a track.

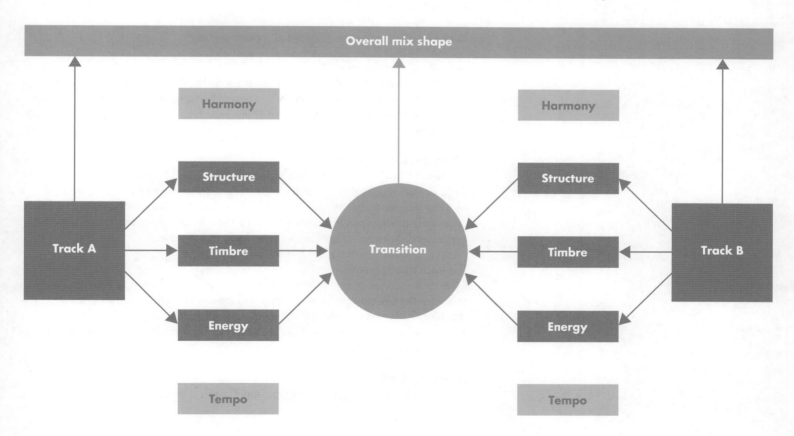

Compare these considerations for Track 1 and 2 to work out how best to transition between them. Don't forget how each track and transition contributes to the overall mix shape.

Harmonic mixing

Basics of harmony

Mixing tracks out of key can sound displeasing and turn a happy vibrant audience into an unsettled one in a short period of time. Whilst as musicians we must learn to trust our ears, we should still build up some solid music theory to help explain what we're hearing. Here's a short course in basic music theory.

There are up to 88 keys on a piano, but there are only 12 different notes. These 12 notes can be grouped together in various ways to create **keys**. The key of C major, for example, contains these notes:
C D E F G A B

While the key of B♭ minor contains these notes:
B♭ C D♭ E♭ F G♭ A♭

Within each key you can play specific groups of notes together (typically three) that are called **chords**. As there are seven notes in a key, you can play seven chords, however there are three that are the most commonly used (made on the first, fourth and fifth notes of the key).

Common chords in the key of C major:
C major = C E G
F major = F A C
G major = G B D

Common chords in the key of B♭ minor:
B♭ minor = B♭ D♭ F
E♭ minor = E♭ G♭ B♭
F minor/F major = F A♭ C / F A C

Almost all electronic music is written in a particular key.

Why does this matter?
Some keys sound good when they are played together, and some do not. As a basic principle, the more notes two keys have in common, the better they will sound. Mixing a track in C major with a track in B♭ minor, for example, may sound bad because there are only two notes in common.

When does this matter?
The type of transition
If you are using a drop in or a straight cut to transition between two tracks, then their keys are less important, because they do not overlap. But if you are performing a bass swap, during which two tracks are played together for a number of phrases, then the keys of each track will affect how well the tracks mix together.

The track's components
If the tracks you are mixing have no melody or chords, i.e. drum kit and percussion only, then the key may not be so obvious and there is less risk of two keys clashing. However, if your tracks contain clear vocals, guitars, pianos, pads or basslines, then the keys will be a prominent part of the music and it is much more important that they fit well together.

Harmonic blending
To blend harmonically, mix together tracks that are in complementary keys.

Which keys work well together and which don't?

The circle of fifths

The more notes two keys have in common, the better they will sound together. The key that is the fifth note of another key is always complementary, because it is the key with the most notes in common with the first key. (In fact, all but one of the notes are the same.)

For example, look at C major:
```
1 2 3 4 5 6 7
C D E F G A B
```

The fifth note is G. Now let's look at G major:
```
1 2 3 4 5 6 7
G A B C D E F♯
```
All notes are the same but one: F♯.

The fifth note of G major is D. D major is made up of the notes:
D E F♯ G A B C♯

Compare D major to G major. What's the difference? (Only C♯.)

The **circle of fifths** tells you how similar two keys are. The further apart the two keys are, the fewer notes they have in common, and the less likely they are to sound good together. As a general rule, try to stay either side of the first track's key.

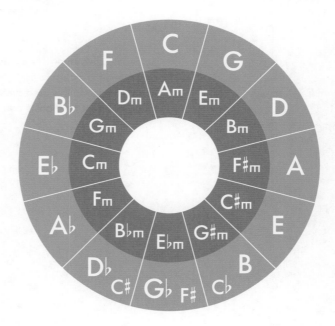

Relative minors

The circle of fifths shows you an outer circle of major chords and an inner circle of minor chords. Major and minor keys come in pairs. Every major key has a minor key that contains the same notes, so you know you can safely mix between, for example, A♭ major and F minor.

If you are playing records, it may help to write the key on the record sleeve.

The Camelot wheel
The Camelot wheel is another system for describing how similar two keys are. Instead of key names it uses numbers and letters. The closer the number is the closer the key. Comparing it with the circle of fifths, you'll notice that 'A' means a minor key and 'B' means major.

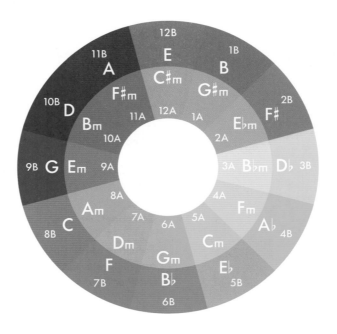

 If you play an acoustic instrument like a piano, guitar or violin, try to listen to your tracks and play the melodies by ear. Once you know the notes in the melodies, you can work out what keys your tracks are in.

Some DJs always mix harmonically, some do not. It is important to be creative here and not just play tracks that 'look' like they will go together. You can really have fun experimenting in this area and yes, sometimes you can put together two tracks with totally different harmonies and vibes.

FutureDJs

Stage: 5

Further techniques

Equipment functions part 3

Here are the new equipment functions you'll need for this stage.

Mixer

1 **Crossfader settings**

As the crossfader moves from one side to the other, it fades out one side and fades in the other. The way in which it does this can be adjusted. There are usually three different options for the crossfader.

Through — Allows signal straight through the crossfader without it being affected.

Cross — Fades in a gradual curve.

Table
Fades in sharply. This is often the preferred setting for scratching.

Some mixers provide a knob that allows you to manually adjust curve between 'cross' and 'table'.

2 **Effect selector**

The way effects are selected and adjusted varies from equipment to equipment. The controls may be found on your software.

3 **Effect on/off button**

Activate the effect with the On/off button. Commonly, once activated, it will flash.

4 **Effect parameters**

Every effect has a set of parameters that can be adjusted, these may include time, beat fraction or percentage.

5 **Effect wet/dry**

The wet/dry knob controls the amount of effect you want to be added to a channel. Completely dry signal contains no affected signal. Completely wet signal contains only affected signal. With the knob in the 12 o'clock position, the signal is split evenly between 'wet' and 'dry'.

6 **Filter**

Turning the knob clockwise creates a high-pass filter: the further you turn, the higher the cut-off frequency. Turning anti clockwise produces a low-pass filter: the further you turn, the lower the cut-off frequency.

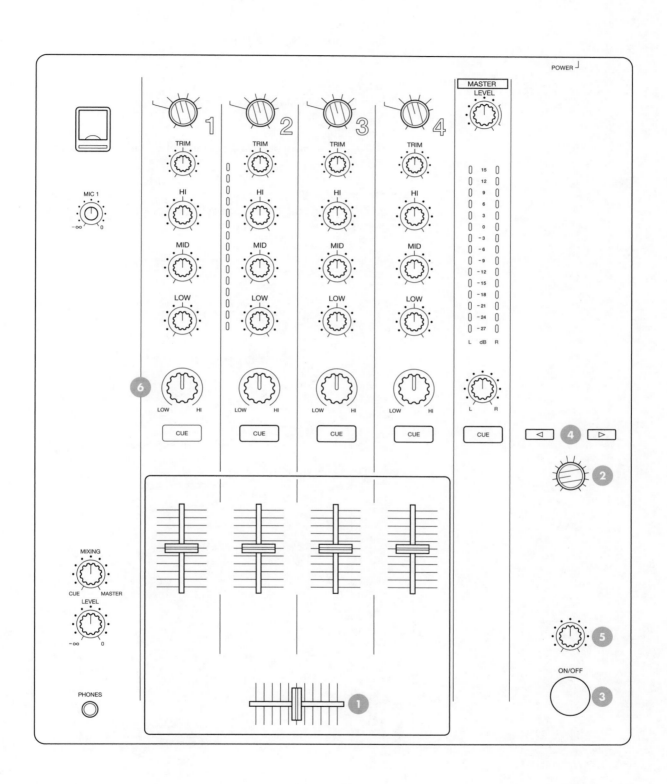

Media player (CDJ)

1 **Loop buttons**

In
Sets the point on which a loop starts.

Out
Sets the point on which a loop ends. Once you hit this button, the track will jump back to the In point and start looping.

Exit/Reloop
Use this to return to loop playback (reloop) or cancel loop playback (loop exit).

2 **Quantise**
The quantise function snaps loop in and out points, hot cues and cues to the nearest beat or fraction of a beat.

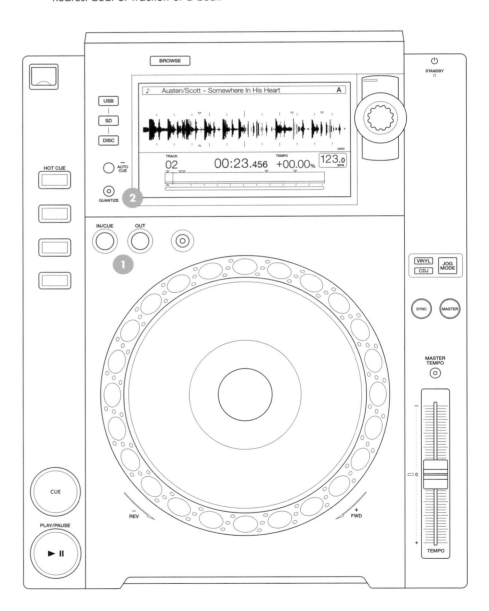

Controller + software

① Effects

② Loop buttons
In
Out
Loop exit

③ Performance pads

On the software:

④ Crossfader settings

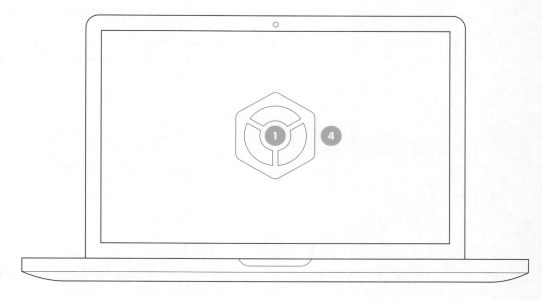

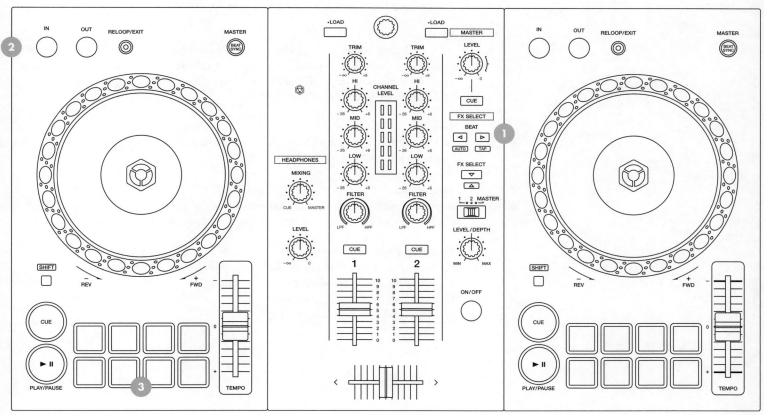

Live editing

One of the fantastic things about modern-day technology and DJ-ing is the possibility of making whole new tracks on the fly. In the next section we're going to look at the tools that DJs can have at the tip of their fingers to edit and manipulate music to their hearts' content.

These are essential skills. Even when executing a meticulously planned set, a DJ must listen intently and be prepared to react to the unexpected and deal with it instantly. The ability to improvise gives a DJ confidence in dealing with any situation and the opportunity to create moments of magic, based on instinct and passion. A lot of DJs will begin a set not knowing where it will take them. They let their music guide them. Just as a jazz musician knows their scales, arpeggios and chords, a DJ knows their music. The selection of music is improvised. The transitions are improvised. The live editing is improvised. This is the very essence of being a DJ.

Looping, effects, hot cues and other features broaden a DJ's control over their music. Technology will continue to advance the capabilities of a DJ.

A cappella

As well as whole tracks, a DJ can use specific, isolated elements of a track as a tool in their mixing. This may include a kick-drum loop, a bassline, sound effects or an a cappella. An a cappella is a vocal without any accompanying music. This can be used in combination with instrumental tracks or instrumental sections of other tracks to create new mash-ups. This is a popular technique in EDM and Hip-hop DJ-ing that can bring a lot of originality to your mix.

(i) **DJ tools**
A cappellas are not the only tool a DJ has in their toolbox. A DJ can also use instrumental tracks, tempo-changing tracks, swooshes...

Tempo
An a cappella does not contain any instrumental or percussive component, so it is much more difficult to feel the tempo of the pulse. It's even more difficult with software. If possible, check the tempo against the original track the a cappella comes from. Always prepare in advance; add the bpm to the metadata.

Harmony
Almost all sung (rather than spoken) a cappellas will be in a specific key, and will therefore use a particular scale. If the notes in this scale are too dissimilar to the notes used in the instrumental track, the two will clash. Check that your metadata is correct, and always mix a cappellas harmonically.

Level
Be wary of the level of the a cappella in comparison to the track you are mixing it with. You want it to feel like it's one track.

Cueing up
Set your cue point or hot cue as you would anywhere else – on the leading edge of the first beat of the sound you want to hear, as accurately as you can.

Pressing play
An a cappella may not begin on the first beat of the bar. It may have an upbeat, known as an anacrusis, which means you may not be pressing PLAY on beat 1. It might be beat 3, or beat 4½. Experiment by starting on different beats and bars; if it's well known, keep to the original placement.

A cappella/Golden (A cappella)
Instrumentals/Golden (Instrumental)

1. Load up **Golden (A cappella)** from the FutureDJs music folder onto Deck 1 and **Golden (Instrumental)** onto Deck 2.

2. ▼ Place a cue-point on the leading edge of the first word of the a cappella.

3. Listen to the a cappella and feel the pulse and the phrasing.

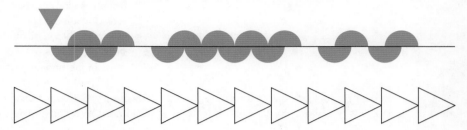

4. Work out where beat 1 of the phrase is. The melody and emphasis on the word 'Golden' tells us that this is the start of the bar and the phrase.

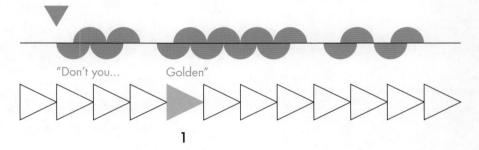

5. Fill in the rest of the beats. Now we know that the a cappella starts on beat 2, three beats before the start of the phrase.

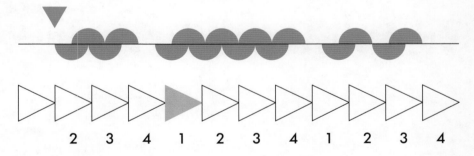

6. Play the instrumental track and trigger the a cappella in phrase and on the correct beat.

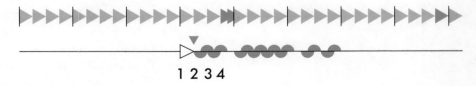

Go through this process with the other a cappellas and instrumentals in the FutureDJs music folder.

Looping

Loops allow a DJ to continually play a section of a track so that it never stops. This is one of the great advantages of digital DJ-ing, giving DJs creative control over the structure of the tracks they use. Loops can also help get you out of sticky situations, for example if your track is about to run out.

A good loop:
— sounds continuous
— does not cut off any components
   (vocals, melodies, chord progressions)
— uses a whole bar or phrase
— uses complete musical ideas
— starts on beat one
— starts at the beginning of a phrase.

💡 If the phrasing is less obvious, shorter loops of 1 bar, or even 2 beats can be very effective.

Always try to loop for one whole phrase, whether it's four bars (16 beats) or eight bars (32 beats). In an emergency, loop two bars (eight beats).

A bad loop:

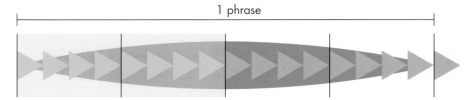

In a track with components lasting four bars, to loop only two bars will jolt the audience and sound like a mistake. Wait for the component to complete its phrase.

This loop is the correct length but does not start on beat one of the bar.

A good loop:

Quantise
The quantise feature will help correct your timing when you punch in and out of a loop.

Looping in outros
There are not many moving components in outros. They are usually percussive (drums only) and don't change too much. This means they can be more easily looped without anyone noticing.

Looping creatively

Any section of a track can be looped, but remember the principles above. A poor loop sounds like a skipping record. A good loop is a creative tool. Here are some examples:

1. **Extend a short intro**
    Intros in Grime, R&B and Hip-hop can often be only one phrase. Use a loop to extend the length of an intro. This gives you more time to mix the tracks together. Play with the EQs, filters and effects to make your transition as effective as possible.

2. **Create your own intro**
    Listen to the track and find a section that can be used as the intro instead. Look for a riff or a cappella in the breakdown. Remember that an intro will only have a few components and few changes, creating frequency space for another track to be layered on top.

3. **Create your own build-up**
    Gradually making a loop shorter and shorter can create momentum and tension. A DJ can use this in combination with a hot cue to create their own build-up and drop.

'My favourite part of DJ-ing is that I get to help break new records. There's no greater satisfaction than getting a demo from an undiscovered producer, playing his record and seeing his reaction. This has been the foundation of my label Saved Records. I feel it's important for us to help develop and nurture the next generation of DJs/producers.'

Nic Fanciulli

Beat-juggling

Beat-juggling is where it all started, with DJ Kool Herc, Grandmaster Flash, and the Hip-hop scene. It was this technique that enabled DJs to extend the break sections of Disco records. By using two copies of the same record on the platters, a DJ could play the break section on one platter and then switch immediately back to the start of the section on the other platter. Now a performance DJ can construct and improvise routines by breaking down existing music and reassembling them into their own rhythms and melodies. Beat-juggling originated on the turntables but can be done on vinyl or digital set-ups. This section gives exercises that can be done on both. The methods of cueing and releasing will vary depending on the equipment, but the principles remain the same.

Markers
As with scratching, on a vinyl set-up, place a sticker on the centre label of the record to mark the beginning of the sample. This helps relocate the start of the sound after the spin back. On a digital set-up, there may be a digital marker on your jog wheel, or you can look at the waveform on the display.

Live looping

2-bar loop on one deck
First try using Deck 1 only, until you feel comfortable with the movements.

1. With the crossfader assigned to Deck 1, play the first 2 bars.

2. On bar 3, beat 1, snap the crossfader to the other deck.

3. Counting 2 bars in your head, spin back to beat 1 and hold.

4. On bar 5, beat 1, release the track and at the same time snap the crossfader back to deck 1.

Repeat this on one deck until the movements are fluent and accurate.

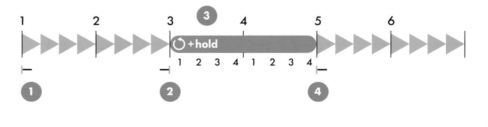

You can find a track in the Beat-juggling folder that's perfect for your practice.

🎧 Beat-juggling

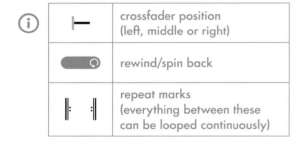

⊢	crossfader position (left, middle or right)	
⬭	rewind/spin back	
‖: :‖	repeat marks (everything between these can be looped continuously)	

2-bar loop on two decks

On two decks, alternate from one deck to the other. As one deck is playing, you are rewinding the other.

1 With the crossfader assigned to Deck 1, play the first 2 bars of Deck 1.

2 On bar 3, beat 1, play Deck 2 and at the same time snap the crossfader across to Deck 2.

3 Rewind Deck 1 to beat 1 and hold.

4 On bar 5, beat 1, release Deck 1 and at the same time snap the crossfader back to Deck 1.

5 Rewind Deck 2 to beat 1 and hold.

Repeat from from step 2.

> To help get used to the timing, on a digital set-up you can use the cue button instead of rewinding the jog wheel.

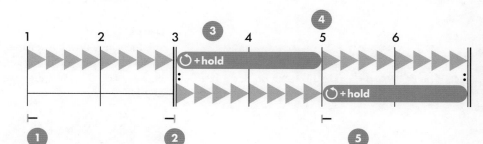

1-bar loop on two decks

Now try to shorten your loop to 1 bar.

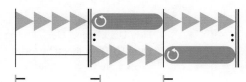

Try looping on beat 2, rather than beat 1. Start Deck 2 on beat 2 and always rewind to beat 2, not beat 1. This will sound the same as looping on beat 1.

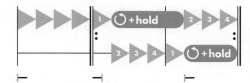

Add a baby scratch

During a 1-bar loop, open the crossfader and add a baby scratch on beat 4.

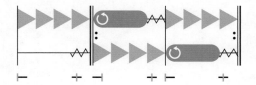

½-bar (2-beat) loop

There's not much time to rewind when the loops get shorter.

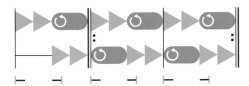

1-beat loop

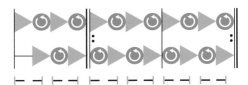

⇄ See **Forward cut/stab** scratch on page 107.

Drops

This technique uses the same technique as the Forward cut. Instead of using a scratch sample however, you are using a component of the beat, like the kick drum, the snare or the hi-hat. Drop in these components whenever you like to create your own variety and syncopation.

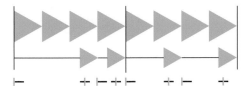

Beat-cutting

Play Deck 1 and Deck 2 a ½ beat apart. Then cut back and forth between Deck 1 and Deck 2 using the crossfader to mix up the beats. You can also try this with Deck 1 and 2 a whole beat or even a $\frac{1}{16}^{th}$ apart.

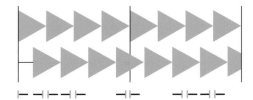

Patterns

Combinations of loops of different lengths and varying the starting beats can completely change the feel and pattern of the beat you are using. This is the real essence of beat-juggling – manipulating existing tracks and turning them into something entirely new.

Try this pattern and then try to create your own.

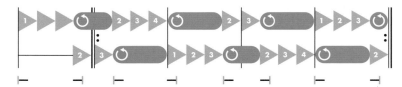

Hot cues

Hot cues allow you to cue up multiple different parts of a track so they are ready to start at the precise point you require. They are like bookmarks — during playback, at the touch of a button, you can instantly jump to an exact point in the track. The method originally came from scratching, where a DJ would mark various cue points on the record, such as the break. Generally, hot cues are a function of digital DJ-ing and are not really applicable to vinyl. They are available on CDJs, controllers and in software like Rekordbox.

Set a hot cue using the same procedure for setting a cue point. A good hot cue is exactly on the leading edge of the beat — the sound must begin the instant the button is pressed.

Setting a hot cue

Navigate to the position in the track using the jog wheel and press a hot cue pad to set a hot cue. Use the waveform and your ears to set your points accurately.

Hot cues as markers

Their most basic use is as markers on the waveform – just as tape was used on vinyl. A hot cue will appear as a boxed and coloured letter above the point of the waveform on which it was set. You may be able to change the colour of the boxes and even name them in software like Rekordbox. As you are learning track structure, they can be used to mark points like:

A = Mix in start
B = Drop 1
C = Breakdown
D = Drop 2
E = Outro

See pages 43 to 45 for a reminder of these symbols

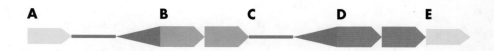

Restructure a track

Hot cues can be used to edit the structure of a track while the track is playing, which allows you to restructure tracks in a live situation and create your own moments. Press a hot cue pad to jump instantly to that point and continue playback. Disable quantise to really test your timing. Enabling it will help you launch your hot cues in perfect synchronisation.

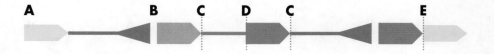

Skip to the second drop

Hot cues can also be used to skip sections. Perhaps your audience isn't reacting to the track in the way you thought they would and you would like to mix out quicker than planned, or perhaps you would like to skip the breakdown to keep the energy high. A hot cue placed on drop 2 can enable you to jump to it at the end of build up 1.

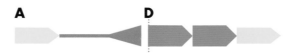

Hot-cue drumming

As well as changing the structure, hot cues enable you to write your own melodies, basslines and drum patterns using sounds within your music. By setting numerous hot cues on different sounds or combinations of sounds, a DJ can jump between them in an order and rhythm of their choice. To be most effective, the key is to find isolated sounds — a single snare hit, kick drum, or note of a melody or a cappella.

Drum patterns

Load up Hot-cue drumming onto Deck 1.
Set the hot cues as follows:

A = Kick drum
B = Snare
C = Hi-hat

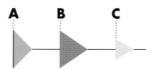

Turn to the back pages and try to replicate the drum patterns shown in the drum racks for each genre. Listen to your own music. Check for exposed drum patterns that could be used for hot-cue drumming.

A cappella

Load up an a cappella from the FutureDJs A cappella folder. Set hot cues at the beginning of words or phrases that you would like to use, for example:

A = "Oo"
B = "are"
C = "you ready"

Signal flow part 3: filters + effects

Some stand-alone mixers have in-built effects, some don't and require external effects units. If you use a laptop in your set-up, you will probably have access to effects within the software you are using. Filters and effects can miraculously change your music at the push of a button, but how and where does the magic happen? There are several opportunities to affect the signal on a mixer.

1 Filter
A filter is commonly placed after the EQs in the signal chain. Typically, turning clockwise will produce a high-pass filter and turning anti-clockwise will produce a low-pass filter.

2 Pre-fade effects
Pre-fade effects are pre-fade because they are before the channel fader in the signal chain. This means that the volume of the affected signal can be controlled by the channel fader. Pre-fade effects include the Filter, and other 'colour' effects like Sweep, Noise, Crush or Dub echo that are also often operated with the Filter knob.

3 Post-fade effects
Post-fade effects are applied after the channel fader. This means that even if the channel fader is closed, affected signal that has already passed through may still be heard.

4 Built-in effects
A built-in effects unit on a mixer will allow you to select from a number of effects. You may be able to choose the channel to apply them to and adjust parameters such as Wet/dry, Time, and Beat fraction.

5 Software effects
On a controller you may have the option to select effects on your laptop and then adjust them using the built-in controls.

6 Send/return
Signal is sent out to a device (most commonly an external effects unit), edited and then returned to the channel (or a different channel).

Analogue

In short (very short), analogue audio signal is a smooth and continuous wave. All sound waves in the natural world are smooth and continuous. The human voice can be said to produce analogue signal. In order for us to hear audio, the signal must become analogue.

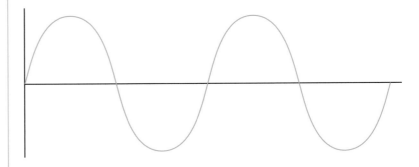

Digital

In order to save or process audio on a computer, however, analogue signal must be converted to digital signal — represented in a sequence of digits that a computer can understand. Because of this, a digital signal is not smooth and continuous, it produces a stepped square wave, where each step is a finite number. In order to play a digital signal aloud, it has to be converted back into analogue signal (by your computer, audio interface or other equipment), before being sent to your speakers.

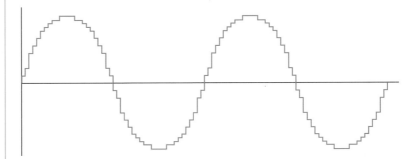

It can be argued that analogue signal that has been converted to digital and back again does not match up to the quality of the original analogue audio. It depends a lot on the quality of the equipment and the sampling rate.

Filters

Filters are such an effective tool for a DJ that mixers and controllers often have dedicated knobs for the job. Filters only let sound through above or below a specified point. They don't boost frequencies, they only cut. There are three types – high-pass, low-pass and band-pass. A DJ will most commonly find high-pass and low-pass filters on a mixer, combined into one knob:

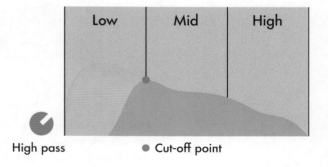

Low pass   High pass

Uses:
— to enhance a build-up
— to create tension leading up to the end of a phrase or section
— to fade a track in or out during a transition
— to balance frequencies between tracks

High-pass filter

This allows sound through that is higher than the set cut-off frequency — it lets the higher frequencies 'pass' while everything beneath is silenced.

Sounds like you are sat next to someone on the train playing music loudly through their headphones.

Low	Mid	High

High pass   ● Cut-off point

Mix in
The high-pass filter very effectively cuts the bass from a track.

Start with the high-pass filter engaged on the in-coming track, around the 4 o'clock position. As you introduce the track into the mix with the channel fader, gradually rotate the knob anti clockwise from 4 o'clock to 12 o'clock to reduce the amount of filter on the track. Experiment with varying the speed and timing of the filter adjustment.

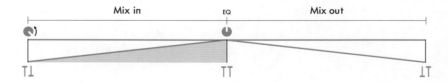

Mix out

A high pass can also be applied to the mix out. It will help your out-going track disappear without a trace. Gradually rotate the knob clockwise to apply the filter and cut the bass out of the mix.

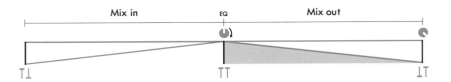

Low-pass filter

This allows sound through that is lower than the set cut-off frequency. The lows are allowed to 'pass' and everything above is cut off.

Sounds like the neighbours are having a party.

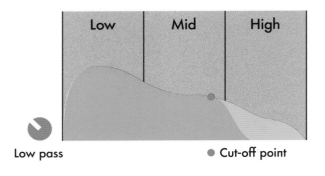

Low pass   ● Cut-off point

 Be mindful of balancing the bass frequencies when using a low pass in a transition.

Mix in

The same technique can be applied to the low-pass filter. Start with the high-pass filter around the 8 o'clock position. As you introduce the track into the mix with the channel fader, gradually rotate the knob clockwise from 8 o'clock to 12 o'clock, to reduce the amount of filter on the track. Experiment with varying the speed and timing of the filter adjustment.

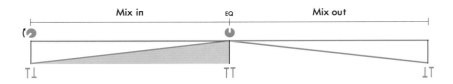

Mix out

Gradually rotate the knob anti clockwise to apply the filter and cut the high frequencies out of the mix.

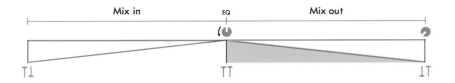

Effects/
EFX/FX

 Revisit **Signal flow part 3: filters + effects** on page 95 to see how this works.

Effects are ways of processing sound, or, literally, affecting the signal. There are various effects available to a DJ — some affect the timbre of tracks, some the rhythm. When used wisely, they can enhance articulation and add a great deal of expression to your mix. Overuse or inappropriate use can spoil the impact of your carefully selected tunes.

Effects are usually either built into a mixer or controller, accessible via software or external units connected via Send/return.

Here are some common effects that you are likely to come across, and effective ways to implement them in your mixing.

Tools for the job:

Effects selector	Effects On/Off	Parameter select	Wet/dry or level knob

(i) You can also select whether you want to apply the effect to a particular channel, or the master.

(i) Effects on a DJ mixer may not operate exactly as they do in a digital audio workstation.

Effects/Delay

Delay

A delay records the input signal and then plays it back after a specified number of beats.

Imagine your shadow following you as you walk. Now imagine you can tell your shadow to walk a step behind you, or two steps or four steps. Your shadow still walks in time with you, just delayed by the number of steps you wish. Delay creates a shadow of the signal delayed by the number of beats that you specify. You can then control how much of the shadow you hear relative to the track itself.

1-beat delay, 25% Wet/dry

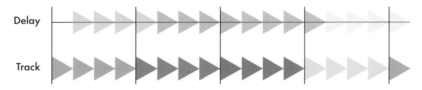

4-beat delay, 50% Wet/dry

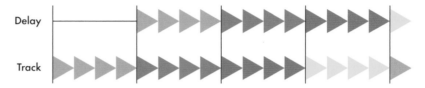

½-beat delay, 80% Wet/dry

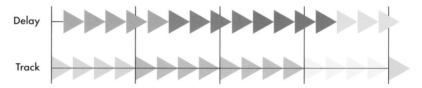

Uses:
— to create movement and energy
— to enhance build-ups
— to edit rhythms and melodies

Echo

The echo effect mimics an echo found in nature. Imagine shouting 'Hello' in a cave and hearing your voice repeat and slowly die away – that's an echo. It's the same sound, again (and again, and again), getting quieter each time until it eventually disappears. It's the same for a DJ: a sound is sampled and played back multiple times, gradually decreasing in volume until it fades away. It is most effective when the track is stopped, so the echo can be heard.

4-beat echo 50% Wet/dry

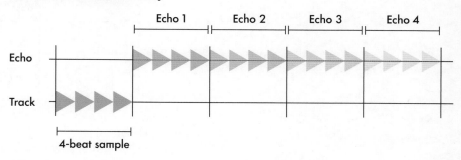

½-beat echo 100% Wet/dry

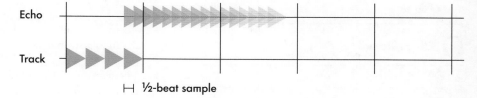

Uses:
— to add layers, texture and movement to an a cappella
— to create a tail in a transition, like a drop in or spin back
— to enhance sparse moments such as in a breakdown
— to smooth a transition between different tempi

'Try not to use too many effects, it can kill the vibe and make sets sound cheap. Learn the basics well first.'

Lauren Lo Sung

Flanger

 Effects/Flanger

A flanger creates a swooshing effect that sweeps up and down the frequency spectrum. Imagine combining your track with the sound of a jet plane repeatedly taking off and landing. You can control how quickly the plane takes off or lands. It is created by mixing the signal with a slightly delayed copy of itself and continuously changing the delay time. The changing delay time affects the pitch, creating the sweeping effect. You can adjust the rate of change from as slow as 16 bars to as fast as a $\frac{1}{16}$th of a beat.

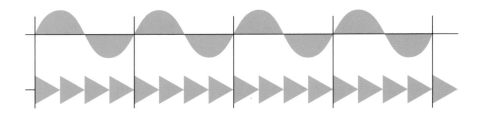

Uses:
— to create your own build-up
— to create movement and momentum

Reverb

Effects/Reverb

Reverb occurs when a sound wave is reflected many times after the sound is produced. Reverb sustains a sound.

Imagine throwing a tennis ball against a wall in an empty room. The ball will bounce from wall to wall and take a long time to come to a standstill. Now imagine throwing a tennis ball in your bedroom. The ball will likely hit various pieces of furniture or a cushion and come to a halt very quickly. It will reflect very little before it stops. It's the same with sound waves. The more surfaces there are, and the softer they are, the quicker the sound will be absorbed and stop altogether. In large spaces like a hall or church, sound waves are able to travel further and last longer before they die away. 'Reverb' creates this effect, adding a decay or a fade-out to the sounds in your track.

Wet/dry

0%

50%

100%

| ▶ | beat |
| ◀ | reverb |

Uses:
— to create a tail in a transition, like a quick fade or spin back
— to increase size and depth of an a cappella or a build-up
— to create your own build-up

The reverb effect is particularly effective when the low frequency has been cut and you begin to apply reverb to the mid and high frequencies.

Scratching

A scratch DJ has an amazing range of sounds at their disposal in any genre, that can be manipulated by changing the length, pitch and rhythm with ease, control and creativity. Scratching may be improvised, made into routines, copied from other DJs, learnt by ear or learnt from notation. It tests coordination, dexterity and feeling for pulse. In this section you will find an introduction to the basic five scratches: baby, chirp, forward cut/stab, transform, flare and drop techniques.

Equipment

Whether it is digital or vinyl, you can scratch if your equipment has a jog wheel and a crossfader. If you are using CDJs or a controller, make sure they are in 'vinyl' mode, or equivalent. If you are using turntables, you may want to use them in battle mode (rotated 90 degrees) so your hands are well away from the tone arms.

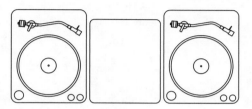

Crossfader

'Open' means the deck can be heard. The crossfader must be either in the middle, or to the side of the deck playing the sound.

'Closed' means the deck cannot be heard. The crossfader is assigned to the opposite deck.

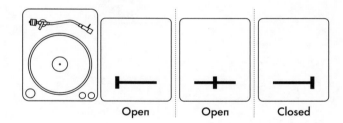

Open   Open   Closed

Crossfader curve

For scratching, adjust your crossfader curve to 'sharp' or 'fast'. You can do this on your software or on your equipment. This means that the crossfader does not need to move far in order to fully output the opposite deck at full volume.

Between the dotted lines, both channels are output at full volume.

'Mastering scratching is like learning karate, you can't become a blackbelt overnight.'

Herschel Lowry (DJ SEBADEE)
FutureDJs tutor

Scratch samples

 These samples were taken from the Fab Five Freddy track Change the beat.

Genres/Hip-hop

Sounds

Any sound can be scratched with, but you will find some more effective than others. Long, sustained sounds are ideal, whether vocal, instrumental or percussive. The most famous and commonly used are:

Ahhhhh   Fressshhh

Beats

A Hip-hop beat is ideal for practising your scratching, but it can be any genre. They are usually instrumentals (no vocals) – scratching becomes the voice.

Markers

On a digital set-up, you may find an LED dial on the jog wheel that shows the rotation. Otherwise, use the waveform and your ears to find the start of the sound.

On vinyl, use stickers to mark the start of the sound relative to the needle.

Hand position

To start with, use your strong hand (usually your writing hand) on the crossfader and the other on the record/jog wheel.

Right-handed

Left-handed

Rest your record/jog wheel hand comfortably at 9 o'clock, then lift your wrist slightly so just your fingers are touching the surface.

Try to keep your crossfader hand rotated outwards so your palm is facing the wall (not the floor) and your upper arm is against your body.

Scratch notation

TTM (Turntablist Transcription Method) is a notation system for scratching. Here we use a simplified version. The horizontal axis is time, and the grid breaks up time into bars and beats. The vertical axis is the amount of the sample you use – the length of the scratch.

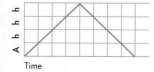

Baby scratch

The baby scratch action forms the basis of all your scratching techniques. All it requires is a simple forward and back movement of your hand on the jog wheel/platter.

1	Place your hand in the 9 o'clock position with your wrist slightly raised so only the pads of your fingers touch the record/jog wheel.	
2	Move forwards a quarter turn…	
3	…and backwards a quarter turn.	

Sounds like:
'duhv-va, duhv-va'

Looks like:

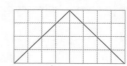

💡 Relax your shoulders, your arm and your hand. Speed and fluidity come from relaxation, not tension. Try it with both hands.

Scribble

The scribble is simple in theory but can be more difficult in practice. Place your fingers on the record/jog wheel and quickly wobble back and forth, creating a tremolo effect. Start slow, stay relaxed and build up your speed.

1	Place your hand in the 9 o'clock position with only the tips of your fingers touching the record/jog wheel.	
2	Wobble quickly back and forth.	

Sounds like:
'wwwwww'

Looks like:

Drop scratch

For this technique, the platter must be spinning or you must have started playback. Instead of pushing the record/jog wheel forward with your hand, simply let go and let the sample play. Then catch it at 12 o'clock and pull it back to the start of the sample, just like the reverse half of a baby scratch.

	Record/jog wheel	
start	Hit PLAY/START Hold the record/jog wheel at the start of the sample.	
1	Release the record/jog wheel to let the sound play.	
2	Catch and draw the record/jog wheel back (like a reverse baby scratch) to the start of the sample.	

Sounds like:
'Ahhh – vvva'

Looks like:

Chirp

A chirp is exactly as you imagine; it sounds like a chirping bird. This technique requires you to use both the record/jog wheel and the crossfader. As the hand on the record/jog wheel performs a baby scratch, the other hand closes and opens the crossfader.

	Record/jog wheel	Crossfader
start		
1	Move your hand forward, using the same motion as the baby scratch.	At the same time, close the crossfader with your other hand.
2	Now move your hand backwards.	At the same time, open the crossfader.

Sounds like:
'Chirp, chirp'

Looks like:

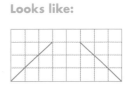

💡 With the crossfader in the middle, push the record/jog wheel forward to play the sound and, at the same time, close the crossfader. The last part of the sample should be cut off. Then, reverse the motion.

Forward cut/stab

The baby and chirp scratches involve two sounds: forward and back. The forward cut, however, is just the forward sound — close the crossfader to cut off the sound before the reverse. For the stab, push the record/jog wheel forward in a short, sharp motion.

	Record/jog wheel	Crossfader
start		
1	Move the record/jog wheel forward.	At the same time, open the crossfader.
2		Close the crossfader.
3	Move the record/jog wheel backwards back to the starting position.	

Sounds like:
'Wi'

Forward looks like:

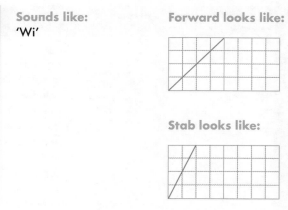

Stab looks like:

💡 The record/jog wheel hand is just doing the baby scratch movement. Be sure to close the crossfader before the backward baby scratch.

Drop cut

With the drop cut, release the sound just like the drop scratch, then cut off the sound by closing the crossfader before the reverse.

	Record/jog wheel	Crossfader
start		
1	Release the record/jog wheel to let the sound play.	At the same time, open the crossfader.
2		Close the crossfader.
3	Catch and draw the record/jog wheel back (like a reverse baby scratch) to the start of the sample.	

Sounds like:
'Ahhh'

Looks like:

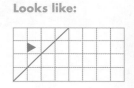

Transform

A transform involves quickly cutting in and out of a sound with the crossfader as your record/jog wheel hand moves forward and back. Long samples work best with transforming.

	Record/jog wheel	Crossfader
start		Apply pressure against the crossfader cap with your thumb to keep it shut. Your thumb acts like a spring.
1	Slowly and steadily move the record/jog wheel forwards.	Tap twice against the other side with your index and/or middle finger to briefly open the crossfader. The thumb will close it again immediately.
2	Move the record/jog wheel backwards.	Tap twice with your fingers

Sounds like:
'Ch, ch, ch, ch'

Looks like:

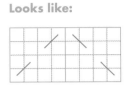

— You should hear a distinctive 'click' as the crossfader opens and closes.
— If you have got the technique then you can start to change the rhythm of the taps and begin to make your own patterns.
— Looping your scratch sample can help you focus on your crossfader hand.

Flare

The flare scratch is the most advanced scratching technique in this book. It opens the door to more combinations and patterns in scratching. The record/jog wheel hand action is the same steady forward and back motion as the transform. The crossfader hand, however, starts open and clicks closed during the forward and backward movement.

	Record/jog wheel	Crossfader
start		
1	Slowly and steadily move the record/jog wheel forward.	With the fader cap between your finger and thumb, make a sideways movement to close and then reopen the crossfader to where it started.
2	Move the record/jog wheel back to 9 o'clock.	At the same time, close and reopen the crossfader.

Sounds like:
'Ah-h-h'

Looks like:
1-click flare

2-click flare

Note that the flare is the opposite of the transform. A transform starts off and clicks on. A flare starts on and clicks off.

Exercises

Try these progressive scratching exercises using the simplified TTM notation. Each page starts with the specified scratch techniques in various rhythms and then introduces previous techniques so you can master your combinations.

Baby scratch

1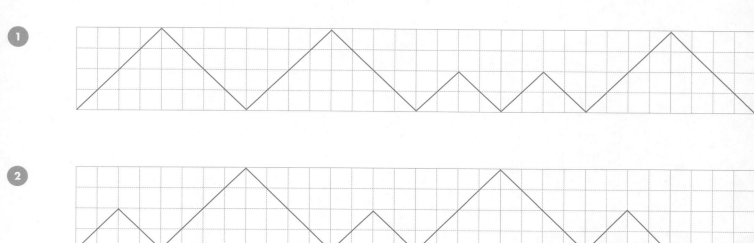

2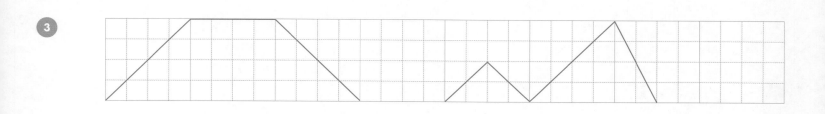

3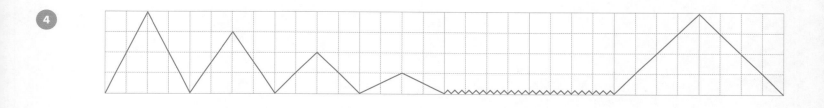

4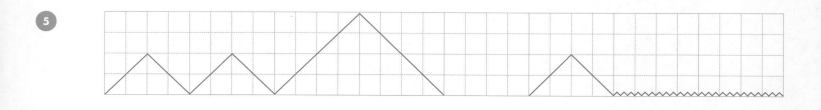

5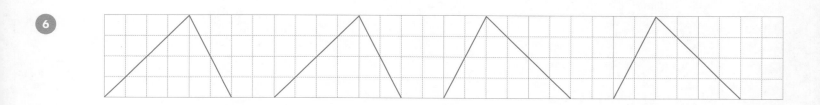

6

Drop scratch

1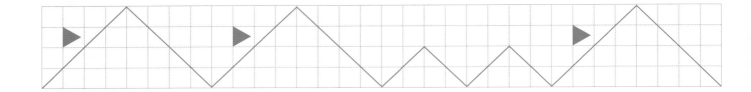

2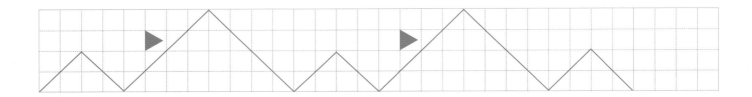

3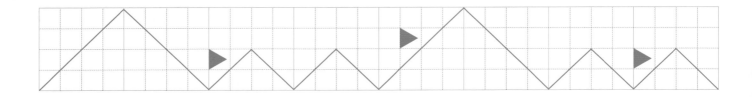

4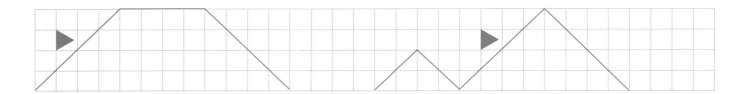

5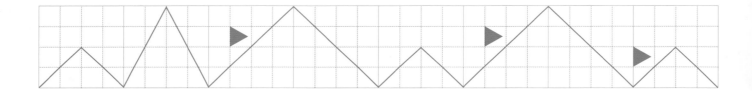

6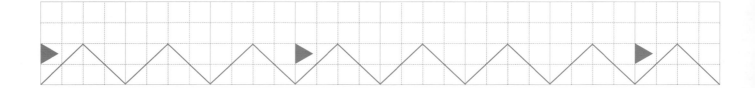

Chirp

1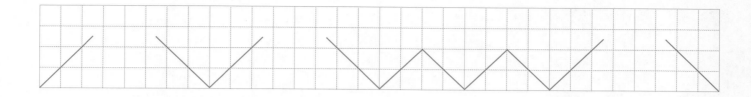

2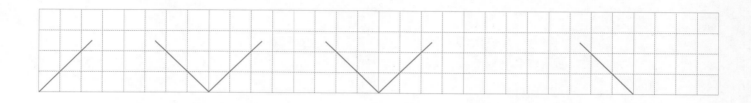

3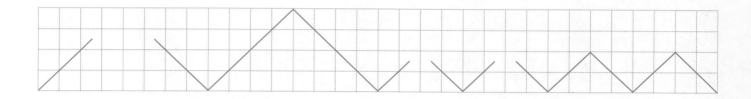

4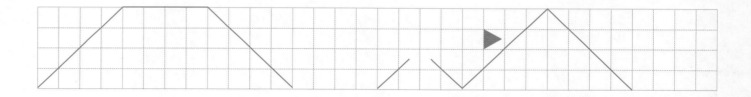

5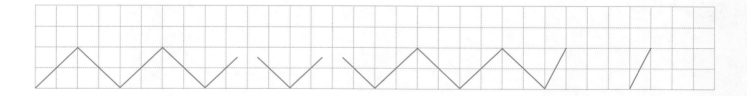

6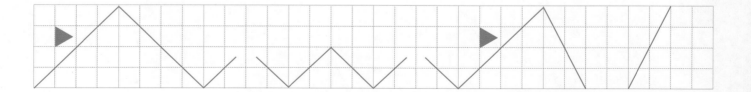

Forward cut/stab

1
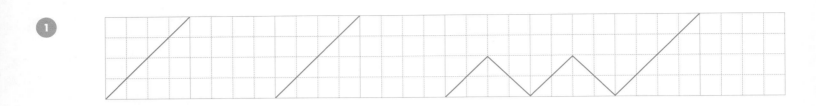

2
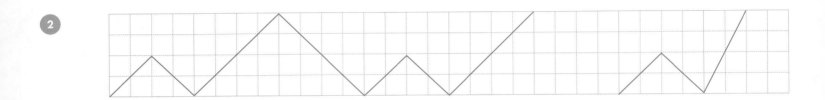

3
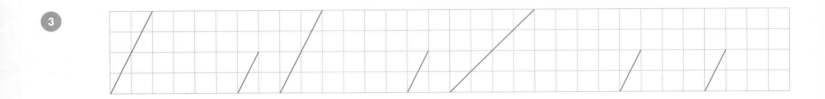

4
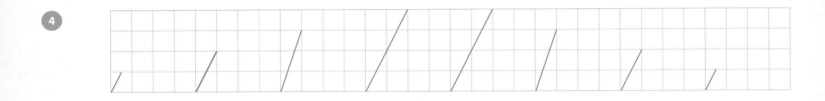

5
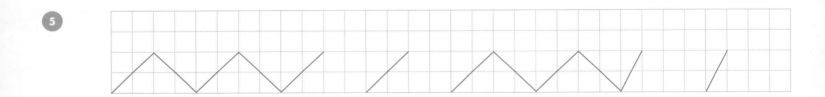

6
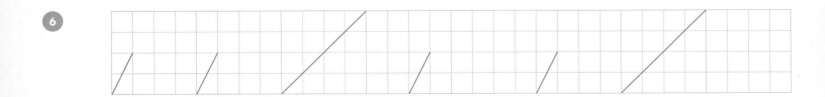

Drop cut

1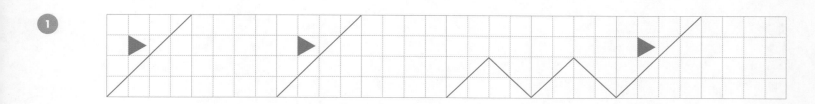

2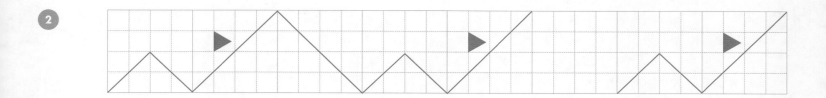

3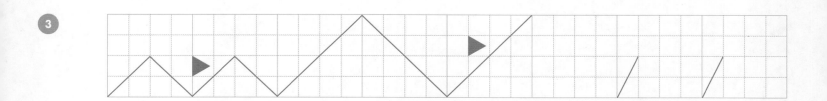

4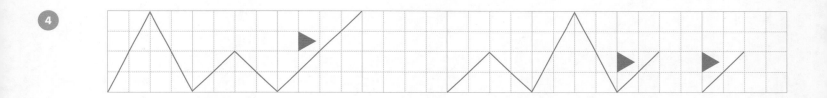

5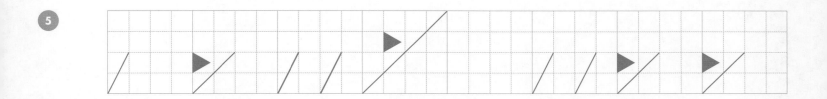

6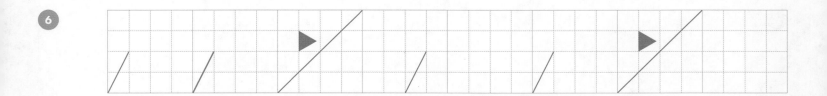

Transform

1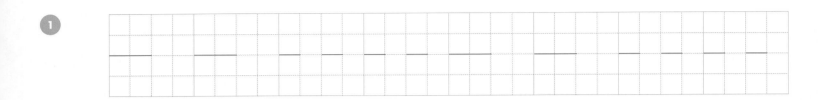

2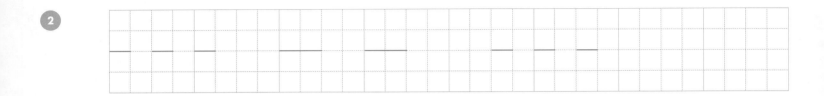

3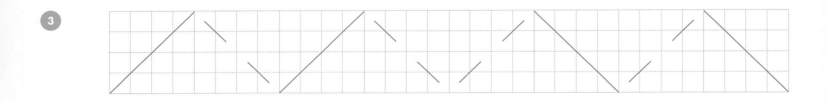

4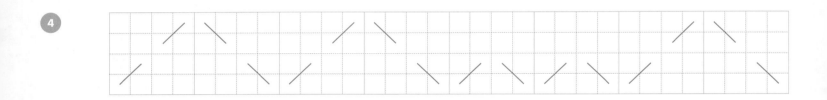

5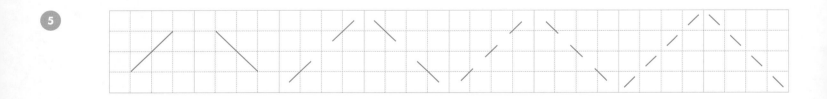

6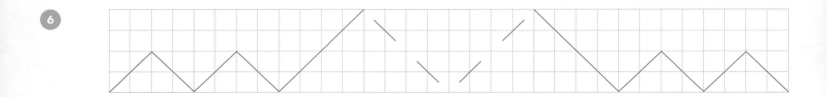

Flare

1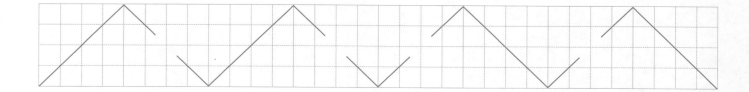

2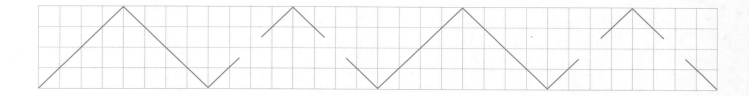

3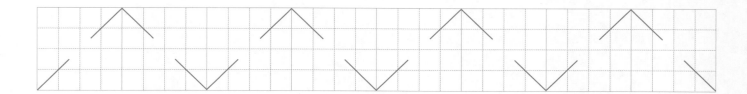

4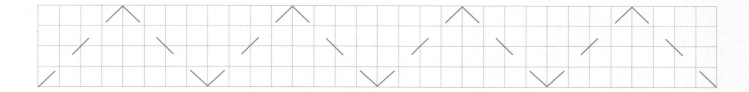

5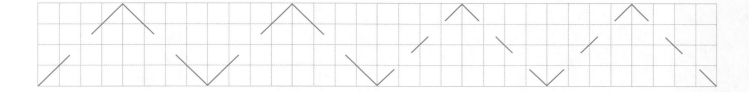

6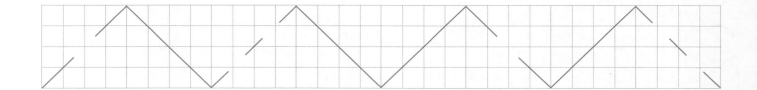

FutureDJs

Stage: 6

Performing

Constructing a mix

A mix is a selection of any number of tracks mixed together into one uninterrupted string of music. They may be recorded for a podcast or played on a radio show. They are usually around one or two hours long and can be completely improvised or meticulously planned. It is a complete representation of a DJ's expression of music at a point in time. It is their composition — a vehicle for their creativity. It is a showcase of their track selection, mixing technique, style and sound, and their preferences for artists, genres, styles and tastes. A DJ may use new tracks, old tracks, their own tracks, samples, tools or any combination. The approach to constructing a mix will naturally differ between DJ-ing cultures and genres. Here are two examples:

1. Structured approach

The structured approach results in a concrete list of tracks in the order in which you will perform them. You may then lay out exactly how you will transition from one to the next using cue points and hot cues.

A framework can help structure our thoughts and limitations, and can encourage creativity, but let the music be the driving force for all your decisions. Follow the direction of your selection of music. The intended effect of a structure will not be achieved if your selection of music does not fit.

Mix shape
The mix shape is a representation of the flow of energy through your mix. Thinking about this can help you map out which kind of tracks you want, and where. You may not end up with the mix shape you intended. Start by answering these questions:

— Do you want your listeners to relax and let their minds wander, or be constantly engaged?
— Do you want to take your listeners on a journey?
— Do you want to entertain your listeners?
— Do you want to surprise your listeners?
— Do you want to conjure a particular emotional reaction, whether it's happy, sad, reflective or excited?

If you would like to excite your listeners and keep them constantly engaged, consider a mix shape that starts low in energy and continually rises:

If the objective is to create a constant energy, then a relatively flat mix may be more effective:

If you want to take them on a journey:

You may want to take note of structural concepts present in other art forms, like the golden ratio, where the mix peaks at the golden number – roughly 60% of the way through. Take a look around you for inspiration.

Track selection

Step 1: Once you have a mix shape in mind, split it into five sections and select tracks that will help you achieve the energy in each section. Gather four or five times the number of tracks you need.

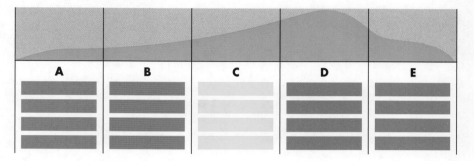

You need to love each one equally; there can be no weak members of the team. Your audience only hears the tracks you play, and not the ones you wanted to play but couldn't make them work in the mix.

Step 2: Pair up your As, Bs, Cs, Ds and Es based on the key considerations for a transition – harmony, tempo, timbre, structure and energy.

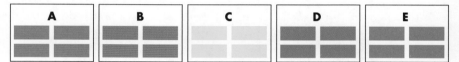

Try mixing them one way and then the other.

Step 3: Then pair up As with Bs, Bs with Cs, Ds with Es. Any combinations that you think may work.

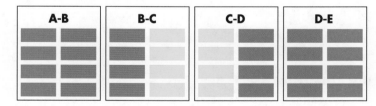

Step 4: Experiment by transitioning between all of your pairs and narrow them down to the ones you like.

'When recording a mix, try to think of a suitable context for it — such as a mix for the poolside on holiday. Having ideas such as this can help the track selections to feel cohesive and give the mix a certain style.'

Manami Baba

Step 5: Find a route through.

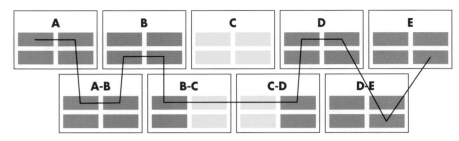

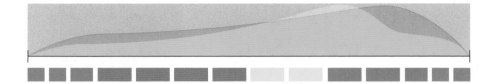

It doesn't matter if the mix shape you end up with is not what you had in mind to begin with.

In practice, this is neither formulaic nor simple. You may realise you need more Ds or Es and have to go back to your collection, or need to search for new tracks because you misinterpreted the energy of a track. Maybe the energy appears to change when placed in a mix. The selection you end up with may not match the mix shape you thought it would, and possibly the mix shape you started with isn't what you wanted. Maybe you actually want to start your mix with a D–E combination.

Regardless, you will have:
— experimented with new combinations
— practised with new tracks
— discovered combinations that work and those that don't
— broadened your collection.

'Try to make to the most perfect, hour-long mix that you possibly can in just one take and then listen back to it properly. If you made some mistakes, what did you do wrong? Were the mixes clashing harmonically in an unpleasant way? Vocals running over each other or some percussion that just didn't fit well? This quest for making the perfect 'mix-tape' will really help you to hone your mixing skills.'

James Zabiela

2. Improvised approach

Improvisation is a skill at the heart of all DJ-ing, and is no less relevant here. It opens up opportunities for unplanned, magical one-time-only moments, fuelled by pure musical instinct. It requires an extensive knowledge of the music in your collection. A quick glance at the title or even just the cover artwork will be enough to remind you of the energy, structure, timbre and even harmony of a track. A DJ will know without listening whether it can be used later in the mix. It also requires an organised collection. Your music management enables you to improvise.

Moments/combinations

The ability to improvise comes from knowledge and confidence. Jazz musicians will know not just their scales and arpeggios, but also riffs, licks and methods of getting from one key to another. Similarly, in order to improvise, a DJ requires both the knowledge of the structures of individual tracks and which tracks in your collection work well together. A DJ will be constructing the mix four or five tracks ahead of what they are currently playing. To improvise is not to be random and out of control, e.g. to be 'winging' it, but quite the opposite.

Mix shape

The mix shape unravels as the mix progresses, and is dictated by how the DJ and audience feels in the moment.

The mix is able to change direction at any moment. What happens in the middle may be decided when it happens. A mix always has a start and an end and a total number of minutes. A DJ will want to end a mix with a sense of completeness, rather than surprise. How you get there may be improvised, but don't lose sight of the end and where you are in relation to it.

'DJ-ing for me is playing music that touches me a lot — from the past, present and future. I often like to play my own edits — music that does not exist in that form on the market. The important thing is to get a sense of the space and how it works: the sound system, the people and the lighting. The creative process starts at the point where I analyze the room and think about what I want to do there, and then I send everyone on a hypnotic journey.'

Ellen Allien

Constructing a routine

A routine is a showcase of skill, creativity, dexterity, mastery of the instrument and compositional technique. It is an art form like no other in that it is judged on the technical ability displayed, the artistry of the performance and the composition of the routine itself. It is an opportunity for scratch DJs to compete with one another; to showcase a new technique, their own ability, their ideas, to communicate, to perform, to push boundaries.

Techniques in a scratch routine generally include scratching, beat-juggling and hot-cue drumming. DJs will utilise beats, samples, a cappella and hot cues, and routines can last from 60 seconds to 15 minutes. There is no formula. Structure, much like in constructing a mix, can help organise your creativity as well as be creative in itself.

Routine structure

A DJ mix is a journey — always moving in a new direction. Think of a routine as being like a story. The pacing and structure of a story affects the impact of the details within it. A good story isn't just about what is told, but the way it's told. A story may centre on a particular character, or an important message. Whether you work from the outside in, or the inside out, the overall form will determine how well your ideas are heard.

Typical structures in music:

A	B

This comprises two contrasting sections. How these sections contrast is up to you — it may be techniques, sounds or complexity etc.

A	B	A1

Like any story, themes and characters develop and return – so can your ideas. A story, however, never repeats itself exactly. There is always a reason for the recap.

A	B	A	C	A

This form keeps returning to a particular idea. As above, it helps to develop the 'A' idea to maintain interest. Consider how the other contrasting sections affect the A sections as they return.

Intro and outro
Adding an intro and outro can frame your routine.

Intro	A	B	A	Outro

Climax
What and where is the climax of your routine? The climax may be the most technically complex section — the most musically intricate, the most impressive, or the most exciting. It is the moment that your routine is building towards – the culmination of all that has come before. As in a DJ mix, the climax is often best left till the final third.

Techniques

Consider separating your routine into sections according to technique. What skills do you have in your armoury? Work with what you know and choose a suitable level of complexity, then divide them into the sections of your routine. Where are your strengths?

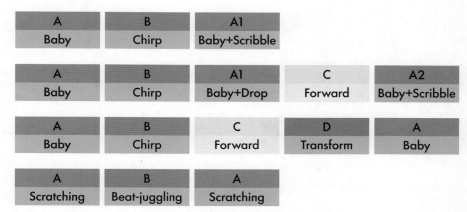

A	B	A1
Baby	Chirp	Baby+Scribble

A	B	A1	C	A2
Baby	Chirp	Baby+Drop	Forward	Baby+Scribble

A	B	C	D	A
Baby	Chirp	Forward	Transform	Baby

A	B	A
Scratching	Beat-juggling	Scratching

It's often good to start simple and get gradually more complex:

Baby	Chirp	Forward	Transform	Flare

Themes

Where does your story take place? Is there a common theme that connects the sections, for example eras of music, genres, artists, music with particular messages or connotations? What does your choice of samples and beats say about you as a DJ and performer?

80s	90s	00s

Jungle	Drum & bass	Scratching

Sounds:

Ahhh	Fresh	Ahhh

What's the moral of the story?

Take a step back from the overall form and think about the point of your routine. What are you trying to achieve? What messages does your choice of music and approach send to others? What are you communicating?

Listen, listen, listen

Ideas rarely spring from nowhere. Research and critical listening will help inspiration strike. Unless you are producing your own sounds, your routine uses music already out there — you have to go find it. You can't make a routine with tracks you haven't heard: so go and listen.

Performing live

'Always respect your audience. Taking chances with music and playing the hits isn't the most respectful thing to do — giving the gig your everything is. Two words that I always swear by are entertainment and enlightenment: you are there to play new music and educate and always always rock it. Play every set as if it is your last.'

Yousef

'Whether you step into an underground club or onto the main stage of a festival, always read the crowd and ensure you have the right three tracks to start your set.'

Mark Brown (CR2 Records)

'I approach each set differently. There are a number of variables that will determine the tracks I select and the direction of my set — venue size, what the DJ before me was playing, how that went down with the crowd and, of course, the mood that I'm in that night.'

Josh Butler

A live mix

Imagine a DJ as a conductor, performing pieces with the power to interpret and manipulate the music as they like. They must be respectful of the music they have chosen. They listen to minute details and sculpt and perfect the sound as it happens. They change pitch, tempo, timbre; they create their own dynamics. While a conductor faces the orchestra, a DJ faces their audience. The audience does not sit still; they show you physically and vocally how much they like your performance — your composition. The feedback is constant and obvious: if they like it, they cheer, applaud and dance, and if they don't like it, they might leave. This presents every DJ with a question: do you play what the audience wants, or what you want? How important is it that your audience likes what you are doing? What if the majority don't like it, but a small minority do? Do you change for everyone else or stick to your guns?

Play what the audience wants ◄————————► Play what you want

Wherever you fall on this scale, and however you have constructed your mix, every FutureDJ must be prepared to change, adapt and improvise.

Preparation

When performing live, there is no substitute for preparation. It's a lot more than just practice:

Music management — Your music management must be up to scratch. You need the ability to access a single track in your collection within seconds. Keep tracks in a system that works for you and fill in your metadata.

Cue points — Check the start of each track. You can slip up if they are inaccurate.

Quantity — Prepare more music than you think you need – much more. Twice as much would be safe.

Hot cues — Place these in consistent positions. Make sure you know what they mean.

Constructing a mix — You know what you are going to do, you have a plan.

Equipment — Have a backup USB stick, and a backup, backup USB stick.

Expectations — Learn about the expectations of your audience, your venue, the DJs either side of you, and yourself.

Things that could affect your mix

However much you prepare, there are countless things that could affect your plans. A live mix is a performance that can never be replicated, even with the same tracks, at the same place, at the same time the next day.

Audience

Regardless of where you fall on the scale above, the audience is why you are there. Remember to look up and see how your music is affecting them. What you do with that information is up to you.

Set-up

Never assume anything about the equipment you are going to be using. Be part of the set-up process if you can, or at least check out what you are playing on before you play. If it's not what you expect, remember that the fundamental functions of every piece of DJ-ing equipment are the same. Keep it simple and improvise.

Venue

The location of your gig, the stage you are on, the room you are in may affect the sound, energy and vibe that is expected of you. Be prepared to improvise.

'I think one of the greatest things about DJ-ing is the way you get to share your favourite music with an audience and see the reaction they give to you and each other. Stylistically, the wonderful thing about sharing this music is that there is only one of you! So you are totally free to express yourself however you feel; after all, no one can be a better you than... you!'

Spencer Parker

Technical hiccups

There are many things out of your control, including equipment malfunctions. The more practice you do, the better prepared you are should anything go wrong.

Mistakes

The music never stops for you; it never slows down to give you more time to think and plan your next move. If you make a mistake, pick yourself up, move on with your set and improvise.

Scenarios

Consider what you would do if:
— The display on your equipment is broken and you have to beat-match every track by ear.
— Your music files corrupt, and you can't perform the mix you have prepared.
— There's a change of plan and you are asked to play Grime rather than House.
— Someone makes a request for a particular song.
— The DJ before you has played half of your selected tracks.
— You miss the play button and your mix-in opportunity is lost.
— The headphone cue isn't working.
— Nobody likes the tracks you are playing.
— You get distracted and have 20 seconds until a track ends.
— There's nobody around and you have to set up the equipment yourself.

A live routine

A live routine is a very different form of performance. After painstakingly shaping your routine through persistent practice, improvisation and experimentation, a live performance is a one-time opportunity to give it the best rendition possible, in front of an audience of your peers. In a competition, it will be judged on technical ability, artistry of the performance and the composition of the routine itself. Just as the DJ techniques in your routine need to be practised, so does the technique of performance. Performing a routine is visual as well as aural. It's not just the details of a story that makes it enjoyable, but the ways those details are brought to life by the storyteller.

Practice

Practice enables you to perform at your very best. It is no different to preparing for a marathon, training your muscles to perform consistently at the standard you want. Here are some tips:
— Work on your technique separately from your routine to help improve consistency.
— Keep a practice diary.
— A small amount of practice every day is more beneficial than lots of practice at one time.
— Be structured and systematic.

Artistry/showmanship

It's more than just a routine – it's a performance. The best routines are not necessarily the most perfectly executed, but they are the most brilliantly performed. A robot could be programmed to execute a routine to technical perfection, however a robot cannot replicate the emotional and physical communication between a performer and the audience.

FutureDJs

Stage: 7

Behind the decks

Joris Voorn

Since a young age I have been obsessed with music. I used to listen to music all day long. At first it was the music my friends were listening to, or my older brother and his friends – mostly music in which guitar played an important role. But when I learned about electronic music I went on a journey by myself — I discovered a new energy in music that literally opened my ears and my mind. I listened to everything, from Trip-Hop to House, Drum and Bass to Techno — even a little Trance in the beginning. Oh, and I was fascinated by Acid, which wasn't really a genre, more a sound created by just one machine, the Roland TB-303.

When I started DJ-ing, all I had were two CD players without a pitch and my small but wide selection of electronic music albums and compilations. With this modest set-up, I miraculously won a minor DJ competition in the local pop venue, which got me my earliest residency as a local DJ on a student night. The first thing I did was buy some cheap turntables and began slowly building up a collection of vinyl records which I practised with in my student room pretty much non-stop.

It was the love of music that pushed me further and further into the world of House and Techno, the two genres that I love most. My deep interest in the art of mixing vinyl records and selecting the right music for the right time made me want to do nothing but DJ-ing. But then I got curious about how all these records were made. At the time there wasn't much on the internet about how to create electronic music, so I just went to the local music store and bought a simple instrument to start learning about music production. That got me hooked, and my teachers at art school started to tell me to focus more on their curriculum. In the end I did finish my education in architecture and design, but I managed to master the art of DJ-ing and a little music production at the same time.

In the long run, it was my love of music that prevailed. It was stronger than my ambition to become a successful architect — I worked in architecture for a short time, but when I managed to get a little success with my first music releases, I decided to go for music full time. It wasn't easy at first, even in 2003 when there wasn't as much competition for DJs and producers, but the power of music was strong and made me persist. The power of music has given me the opportunity to see the world, travel as a DJ, play my music for thousands and meet people in far-away places.

If you love music as much as I do, there's a chance you can make it too, but it's hard work and it takes time. Technically, it's much easier to become a DJ these days, but the need to really embrace the music hasn't changed.

Mr Switch

My interest in DJ-ing began at the peak of UK Garage music, which dominated the charts in the early 2000s. It stood out to me — electronic beats, crazy rhythms, heavy basslines, with DJs and MCs replacing guitarists and boy bands. I was having guitar lessons at the time, but I didn't feel much passion for it or feel particularly skilled at it either. I was still enjoying listening to music, and I yearned to somehow create or play music of my own. I can't remember when I first discovered scratching and turntablism, but there were enough music videos in the charts at the time that featured a DJ to pique my interest. Some had a scratching solo, featured a DJ or group of DJs. It felt like there was a whole other world popping into the spotlight.

When I was 12 my dad bought me a video — the DMC UK DJ Championship — and it blew me away! This was a competition where the best scratching won you the crown and the winners were featured on the DVD cover. Hands flew over faders, records were magically spun into brand new beats and the crowd went crazy! It was Hip-hop, it was underground, it was like Narnia! I had found the world I was looking for — and I wanted to discover more.

I borrowed my parents' turntable and tried to buy the records from the videos. I attempted to copy the moves from the video — I had to know how they were doing these amazing tricks! It seemed superhuman — but also not, at the same time. Because it was just moving records with your hands, I thought I might be able to do it too, with practice. At the time I couldn't imagine entering the competition. Fast forward 17 years and I have won the world championships four times, travelled the world making a career out of DJ-ing — and have made it onto the front of the DVD cover! My 12-year-old self would never have believed it.

I was self-taught for the first two years. I learned from a couple of other local, more experienced DJs. It's amazing how much easier it is to learn, teach and share knowledge these days — as exemplified by this book. Winning DJ competitions was the way I made my name and was a great way of learning, seeing the latest tricks and gaining experience. Part of my success has been my versatility — I play a lot of different genres live, so I can play at all kinds of events and being able to scratch means I can interact with other musicians — bands, beatboxers and orchestras.

Work out what can make you stand out from other DJs and follow every opportunity, you never know where it might lead. What started as a small one-off show led to me becoming the first DJ to perform at the BBC Proms. Be professional and amiable to promoters and agents — so they think of you for their next event. Pick a good name! A lot of people have called themselves DJ Switch, which has led to confusion over the years, hence why I eventually changed to Mr Switch. With DJ-ing, you are a one man band — you can play any instrument and create any kind of sound. Every time you play a set you create a unique, one-off performance that will never be repeated. You're in control of the party and should enjoy the journey.

DJ Mark One

I discovered my love for music and DJ-ing during the first week of the summer holidays in 1987 (I was 14 at the time). Unbeknown to me, I lived next door to a regional DMC mixing champion. One morning he was practising — he had set up his Technics turntables and mixer along with a huge sound system in his back garden. It was the most amazing thing I had ever seen and heard. He was mixing and scratching records at lightning speed and the sounds coming out of the speakers had an amazing effect on my synaesthesia (I see music as a colour spectrum). From that moment onwards, all I ever wanted was to be a DJ.

As I didn't own any turntables at the time, my practice consisted of placing a drum from an old drum kit either side of my four-channel mixer and imitating the DJs on the DMC world finals videos. When I did finally convince my parents to purchase some Technics SL-1210 turntables, mixing and scratching felt natural. I spent the next two years locked away in my room, practising to enter the regional DMC heats, only coming out of my room to attend school and to go to the record shops in Manchester to add to my record collection.

I entered my first DJ competition in 1991 — it didn't go well. But I knew not to expect to win, I was up against DJs who had far superior skills that I couldn't compete with at the time. I was there to prepare myself for the next year's competitions — I suppose you could call it market research. Hundreds of hard, determined hours of practice later, I would go on to win regional mixing championships in multiple competitions for the next three years in a row.

Winning these competitions led to me laying down scratches for a Manchester Hip-hop label called Grand Central Records, who were remixing Europe's biggest-selling band at the time, a band called Texas. From there, I was asked to perform with the band on tour, radio and television promotions for the following 11 years.

That provided me with the opportunity to travel all over the world, playing gigs such as Glastonbury main stage, Top of the Pops and the Brit Awards. We even supported Madonna and many other high profile shows during the height of the 'Brit Pop' era. I had achieved my childhood goals at the age of 24 — I always dreamed of performing on Top of the Pops and at Wembley Arena.

Now, I am teaching and inspiring the next generation of DJs to be expressive, creative, and focussed on this wonderful art form with endless possibilities. We all have the ability to achieve anything we want to in life. Taking the first step towards those goals can be the hardest step to take, but if you are passionate and driven in your pursuits, anything is possible.

FutureDJs **Stage: 8**

Genres

House

Sub-genres
Deep House
Hard House
Electro House
Progressive House
(and many more)

Origins	Tempo	Pioneers
Chicago	118—135 bpm	Tom Moulton
UK		Larry Levan
1980s		Frankie Knuckles
		Jesse Saunders

Defining characteristics

— Positive and upbeat mood
— Written in major keys (though not exclusively)
— 4/4 time signature
— Kick drum on the beat
— Hi-hats on the off-beat
— Claps/snares on the 2nd and 4th beats of the bar
— Synthesized melodies, chords and baselines
— Vocals feature as short repeated samples, catchy hooks or full melodic lines

Typical structure

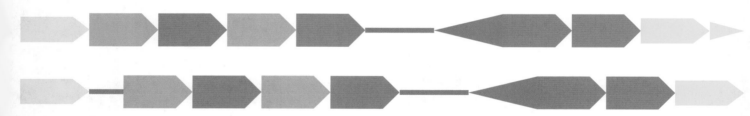

Drum rack

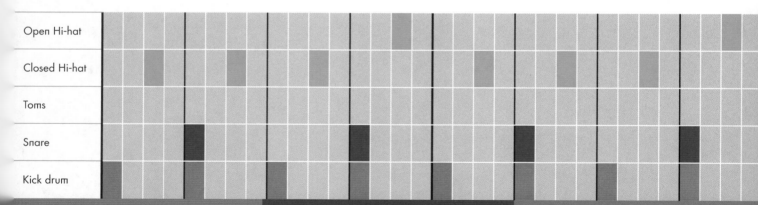

Open Hi-hat	
Closed Hi-hat	
Toms	
Snare	
Kick drum	

Check out

Show Me Love — Robin S
Where Love Lives — Alison Limerick
One More Time — Daft Punk
Lady (Hear Me Tonight) — Modjo
Gypsy Woman — Crystal Waters
Rhythim Is Rhythim — Strings of Life

Record labels

Defected
Toolroom
Nervous
Cr2 Records
Aus Music
Get Physical
Strictly Rhythm

According to Caolan Savage (Nautica)

House music is all about joy. It's almost impossible to listen to a House track, new or old, and not have a smile on your face. The self-expressive nature of the music allows you to truly be yourself — it's a spiritual thing. Stay true to yourself as an artist and you'll go far.

Tech House

Origins	**Tempo**	**Pioneers**
London	120—124 bpm	Terry Francis
1994		Mr C
		Mr G

Defining characteristics

— Combines the swing and bounce of House with the toughness and mood of Techno
— Dubby, tribal, percussive samples on loop
— A lot of groove
— 4/4 time signature, kick drum on every beat, clap/snare on the 2nd and 4th beats
— Short, repeated basslines
— Few harmonic elements or melodies
— Vocals are spoken words or phrases

Typical structure

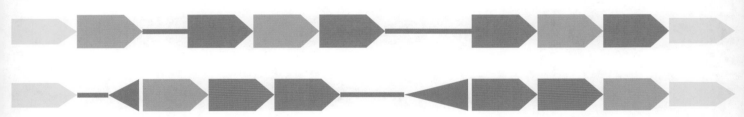

Drum rack

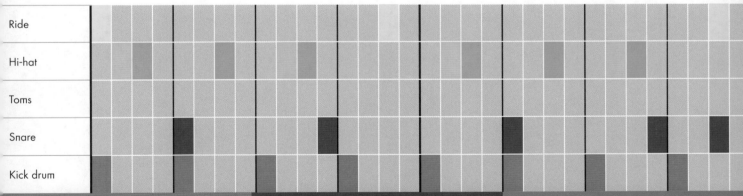

Check out

Be Sharp Say Nowt — Patrick Topping
Hello, Acid Dathera — Terry Francis
Grey — Kølsch
Superfreak (Freak) (Mr. G Remix)
   — Josh Wink
Body Language
   — M.A.N.D.Y. vs. Booka Shade
India In Me — Cobblestone Jazz

Record labels

Hot Creations
Sola
Toolroom Trax
Elrow Music
Stereo Productions
Glasgow Underground
Danse Club
Rejected

According to Carly Newman, FutureDJs tutor, Tech House is Techno and House combined. The 'Tech' part is the thumping bassline and the 'House' element is the hook, the identity of the track that makes it stand out — usually resulting in a banger!

Techno

Sub-genres
Minimal Techno
Dub Techno
Detroit Techno
Industrial Techno

Origins
Detroit
1980s
Berlin

Tempo
125–140 bpm

Pioneers
Juan Atkins
Kevin Saunderson
Derrick May (Belleville three)
Underground Resistance
  (Jeff Mills, Mike Banks, Robert Hood)

Richie Hawtin
Jeff Mills
Joey Beltram
Carl Cox
Kraftwerk

Defining characteristics
— Powerful, dark and mechanical in mood
— Often in minor keys
— 4/4 time signature, kick drum on every beat
— Syncopated percussive layers that interact with each other
— Slowly evolving textures
— Eerie soundscapes and white noise

Typical structure

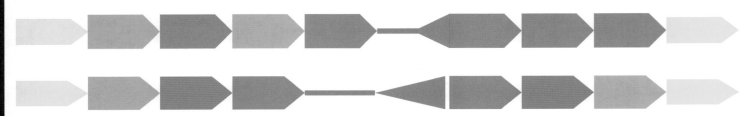

Drum rack

	Ride
	Hi-hat
	Toms
	Snare
	Kick drum

Check out
The Bells — Jeff Mills
No Way Back — Richie Hawtin
M04A — Maurizio
Pacific State — 808 State
Your Mind — Adam Beyer

Record labels
Plus 8
R&S Records
Semantica
Axis Records
Tresor Records
Transmat Records
Metroplex
Drumcode

According to Abstract Man, Techno is a celebration of the beauty of originality and the power of people unified by shared values and beliefs. In its truest form, it encompasses freedom, unity, openness and connection. Techno can ground us: finding meaning and calm in the rhythms, strength and stability in the low frequencies and connection to ourselves, our challenges and each other.

Disco

Origins	Tempo	Pioneers
New York 1970s	110—118 bpm	Donna Summer Gloria Gaynor Sylvester Chic Giorgio Moroder Patrick Cowley

Defining characteristics
— Upbeat, vibrant and happy
— Latin rhythms
— Live orchestral records
— 4/4, kick drums on every beat, claps/snares on the 2nd and 4th beats
— Strong groove, shuffle and swing
— Early electronic synthesis from instruments like the infamous Moog
— Inspired by Motown, Philly funk

Typical structure

Drum rack

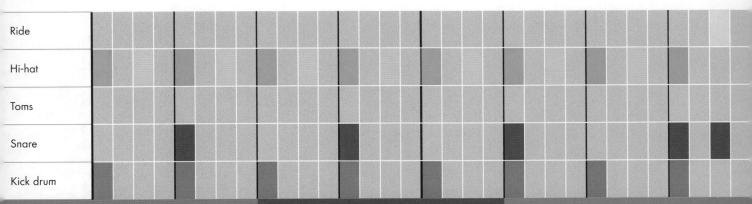

Ride	
Hi-hat	
Toms	
Snare	
Kick drum	

Check out
Disco Inferno — The Trammps
Le Freak — Chic
I Feel Love — Donna Summer
Got To Be Real — Cheryl Lynn
Don't Stop 'Til You Get Enough
 — Michael Jackson

Record labels
Salsoul Records
Philadelphia International Records
Casablanca Records
Motown Records
Prelude Records
20th Century Fox Records

According to DJ Matt Bailey, FutureDJs tutor, Disco isn't just music, it's a feeling. It has the ability to pick you up, make you dance, and put a smile on your face!

Hip-hop/Rap

Origins
Kingston, Jamaica
New York
Los Angeles

Tempo
85—95 bpm

Pioneers

DJ Kool Herc
Africa Bambaataa
Ice-T
Dr. Dre
2Pac
Snoop Dogg

Eminem
The Notorious B.I.G.
Kendrick Lamar
Outkast
Kanye West
50 Cent

Jay-Z
A Tribe Called West
Nas
Wu-Tang Clan

Defining characteristics

— Short, sampled, instrumental hook from soul, funk or jazz music
— Heavily compressed basslines
— Syncopated drum patterns
— Lyrics are sung, spoken, rapped, or shouted
— Rappers take turns to spit their own lyrics over the track
— Meaningful lyrics about the rappers' lives

Typical structure

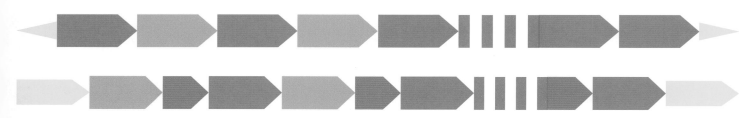

Drum rack

Open Hi-hat															
Closed Hi-hat															
Toms															
Snare															
Kick drum															

Check out

Lose Yourself — Eminem
Changes — 2Pac
Juicy — The Notorious B.I.G.
The Message — Grandmaster Flash
                and the Furious Five
Rapper's Delight — The Sugar Hill Gang
Don't Believe The Hype — Public Enemy

Record labels

Def Jam Recordings
Tommy Boy Music
Bad Boy Records
Death Row Records
Aftermath Entertainment

**According to Joe Mann,
FutureDJs tutor,** Hip-hop is a genre that
has rocked the dance floor for decades,
it has been well and truly tried and tested.
It has its own funky attitude that just seems
to make people groove, and catchy vocals
and raps that nobody ever seems to forget.

Grime

Origins	**Tempo**	**Pioneers**	**Second wave**
London	135—140 bpm	Pay As You Go Cartel	Novelist
2000s		Wiley	Stormzy
		Dizzee Rascal	
		Slimzee	
		Skepta	

Defining characteristics
— Complex, syncopated 2-step (half-time) breakbeats
— Futuristic synthesized leads
— Dark, grungy basslines
— Spoken lyrics about social circumstances and politics
— African dialects and new slang

Typical structure

Drum rack

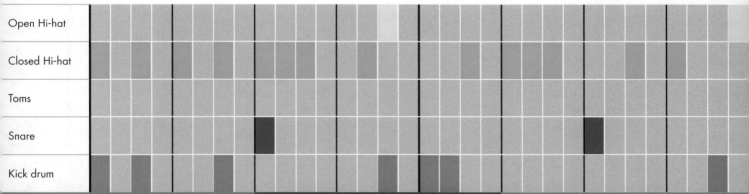

Open Hi-hat																
Closed Hi-hat																
Toms																
Snare																
Kick drum																

Check out
Pow! (Forward) — Lethal Bizzle
When I'm 'Ere — Roll Deep
I Luv U — Dizzee Rascal
P's and Q's — Kano
Wot Do You Call It? — Wiley

Record labels
Boy Better Know
Butterz
Rinse
XL Records
No Hats No Hoods

According to Plastician, Grime is the melting pot of urban living and electronic music. It came about fusing Jamaican sound system culture with British mainstay movements that evolved out of Jungle. DJs playing dark instrumental garage spun tracks for MCs to lace with bars about growing up in London's streets. Sonically and lyrically it embodies the attitudes of UK's youth culture.

Trap

Origins
Atlanta
1990s

Tempo
140 bpm

Pioneers
Outkast
Waka Flocka Flame
T.I.
Jeezy
Gucci Mane
Three 6 Mafia

Drill
67
Loski
Youngs Teflon

Defining characteristics
— Short bursts of rapid-fire hi-hat rhythms
— Half-time beat
— Big, clear, booming basslines
— Long decay on kick drums
— Rap with a triple-time flow
— Dark, eerie sounds
— Bleak lyrics about a life of poverty and crime
— Background vocals with plenty of delay

Typical structure

Drum rack

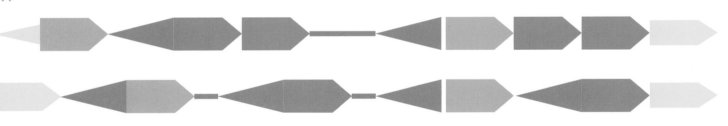

Ride																														
Closed Hi-hat																														
Toms																														
Snare																														
Kick drum																														

Check out
DJ Turn It Up — Yellow Claw
Crowd Ctrl — Flosstradamus
Express Yourself — Diplo
Lean On — DJ Snake and Major Lazer
Trap Queen — Fetty Wap

Record labels
Mad Decent
Astralwerks
Dim Mak
Fools Gold
Never Say Die Records
Monstercat

According to FutureDJs, Trap is fierce and high energy. Hi-hats rattle, snares crack and kick drums jolt and skip. The bass is powerful, the vocals are gritty and drops will make you move.

Garage/2-step

Sub-genres
US Garage
UK Garage
2 Step
Speed Garage
Bassline

Origins	Tempo	Pioneers
London 1990s	120—135 bpm	Todd Edwards Roger Sanchez MAW (Master at Work) MC Creed MJ Cole

Defining characteristics

— 2-step beats
— Irregular, 'broken' (syncopated) kick drum rhythms
— Heavily distorted basslines
— Led by MC crews
— Sampled vocals that are time-stretched and pitch-shifted
— Soulful and classy

Typical structure

Drum rack

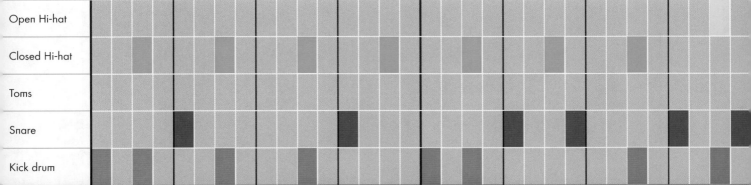

Open Hi-hat		
Closed Hi-hat		
Toms		
Snare		
Kick drum		

Check out
Movin' Too Fast — Artful Dodger
RIP Groove — Double 99
Run To Me — Shola Ama
Spin Spin Sugar — Sneaker Pimps
Flowers — Sweet Female Attitude

Record labels
Hemlock Recordings
Locked On
Big Apple Records
Rinse Recordings
Idle Hands

According to Ollie Weeks, FutureDJs tutor, Garage is the best genre on the planet — it's the sound of the UK. It's a movement of soulful vocals and stabby chords alongside big bass sounds and swinging hats. You can mix Garage at speed, cutting and switching. It's fast, energetic and groovy — what's not to love!

Trance

Sub-genres
Euro Trance
Goa Trance
Hardstyle
Progressive Trance
Psy Trance

Origins	Tempo	Pioneers
Goa	125—150 bpm	Laurent Garnier
		DJ Dag
		Paul van Dyk
		Sasha
		John Digweed
		Armin van Buuren

Defining characteristics
— Anthemic and epic
— Powerful, punchy drum beats
— Lengthy, extended breakdowns leading to big build-ups and euphoric drops
— Tuneful, rising synthesized melodies that make you want to put your arms in the air
— Flangers, phasers, chorus, reverb and delay used to increase the size and intensity of the sound
— Easy-to-sing lyrics on topics of love, happiness, dancing and heaven

Typical structure

Drum rack

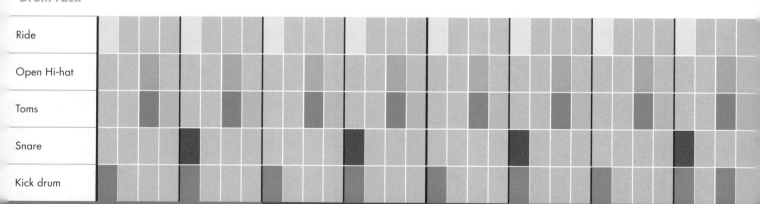

Ride
Open Hi-hat
Toms
Snare
Kick drum

Check out
Armin Van Buuren — Blah Blah Blah
Tiesto — Red Lights
Café Del Mar — Energy 52
Silence — Delerium
For An Angel — Paul van Dyk
Saltwater — Chicane
9PM (Till I Come) — ATB

Record labels
Armada Music
Anjunabeats
A State of Trance
Black Hole Recordings
Silk Music

According to James Hiett, A&R Manager, Armada Music, Trance is dynamic, energetic and full of emotion. Spine-tingling melodies, pounding basslines and crisp percussion all fuse to create an atmosphere on the dance floor like no other. More than 20 years after being exposed to it, I'm as passionate about it as ever — and that is down to its magical aura.

Jungle/Drum + Bass

Sub-genres

Darkcore	Neurofunk
Drumstep	Breakcore
Jazzstep	Jump Up
Liquid	Tech Step

Origins
London
1990s

Tempo
160—180 bpm

Pioneers
Fabio
Groove Rider
Goldie
Roni Size
Adam F
Andy C

Defining characteristics

— Fast, intricate breakbeats
— Dominant, often distorted bass and sub-basslines
— Simple, singable melodies played on synthesizers
— Short, repeated sampled lyrics
— Rhythmically complex and varied drum fills
— Extended breakdowns, where the drums drop out completely
— Long build-ups

DJ-ing techniques
Double drops

Typical structure

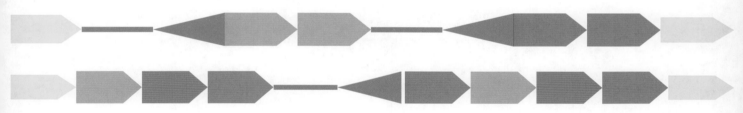

Drum rack

Crash																						
Open Hi-hat																						
Toms																						
Snare																						
Kick drum																						

Check out
Renegade Snares — Omni Trio
Original Nuttah — Shy FX
Brown Paper Bag — Roni Size/Reprazent
Inner City Life — Goldie
Nobody To Love — Sigma

Record labels
Metalheadz
Urban Takeover
Exit Records
Good Looking
Hospital Records
RAM Records

According to Deen Nauthoa (DKN), FutureDJs tutor, Drum & Bass is a forward-thinking genre, deeply steeped in culture, emerging from the early 90s' Jungle scene. It is a true melting pot of inspiration from every musical source imaginable — the diversity of styles is unparalleled and that is no doubt one of the reasons for its ever-increasing popularity.

Dubstep

Origins
London
late 1990s

Tempo
70—75 bpm
(can also be counted
twice as fast
i.e. 140—150 bpm)

Pioneers
Skream
Benga
Kode9
Zed Bias
El-B

Defining characteristics
— Big, powerful, wobbling sub-basslines
— Dark, moody atmospheres
— '2-step' or 'half-step' beats
— Shuffling Hi-hat rhythms, often syncopated and in triplets
— The full range of the frequency spectrum is filled with pads and synths with plenty
  of effects and filters – it's a big wall of sound
— The lowest frequencies are dominated by the sub-bass, rather than the kick drum

Typical structure

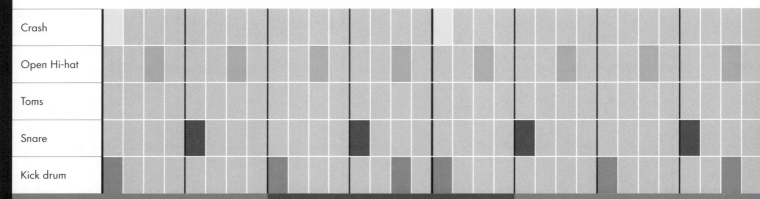

Drum rack

| | Crash | Open Hi-hat | Toms | Snare | Kick drum |

Check out
Bass Cannon — Flux Pavilion
Bangarang — Skrillex
Night — Benga & Coki
I Need Air — Magnetic Man
Louder — DJ Fresh

Record labels
Tempa
LS2
Aus Music
Hotflush Recordings
Chestplate

According to Eloki, Dubstep has a raw and powerful tribal energy that captivates dancers and aligns them in a hypnotic, two-step dance in a common appreciation for music and life.

Commercial

Commercial is not a genre as such — it describes the popularity of a track with regards to its position in a sales chart or a radio stations playlist. The term Commercial covers all genres of music from Rock 'n' Roll to Rap to Drum and Bass. The popularity of a track will have a heavy influence on its structure.

Restrictions on track length and vocal content were enforced in the 1950s with the invention of the transistor radio by Sony. This was the only way people could consume music without purchasing vinyl. Commercial (pop) music was pressed to a 7 inch vinyl format and could only accommodate 4 minutes of music. Sales reports from national distributors formed the creation of the national sales chart in 1952.

Historically, commercial music has influenced generations of fans with its fashion trends, political views, cultural change and it continues to do so to this day. Each decade of commercial music has propelled its most popular artists into household names with the help of huge marketing budgets from major record labels who sign and develop the artists.

Some of the biggest pop stars:
1950's – Elvis Presley
1960's – The Beatles, The Monkees
1970's – Pink Floyd, The Jacksons
1980's – Madonna, U2
1990's – Whitney Houston, Mariah Carey
2000's – Beyoncé, Eminem
2010's – Ed Sheeran, Adele

EDM

EDM (Electric Dance Music) means different things to different groups of people. For some, it defines one of many dance music cultures, rather than a genre itself. EDM culture is centred around popular festivals, clubs and the radio. EDM music fits this culture by providing accessible, high-energy tracks that are fun and energising to listen and dance to. They are instantly enjoyable and easily accessible. The tracks may have stylistic roots in a variety of genres, from House and Techno to Drum and Bass and Dubstep.

There are, however, some defining characteristics:
— Builds and drops
— Electronic, synthesized sounds, using saw waves
— Powerful, euphoric risers
— Tension and release
— Short, memorable vocal phrases

Underground

The term underground is used to describe music not written for the intention of mainstream consumption and widespread popularity. Artists 'in the underground' prioritise musical expression, innovation, experimentation and individuality. Without concern for popularity, artists are free to experiment and push boundaries without fear of their music not being universally well-received. New trends, sounds and genres are often born in the underground that then in time influence commercial music. Every genre has its underground scene.

Other genres to check out

Ambient	Future Bass	IDM (Intelligent Dance Music)
Downtempo	Glitch/Glitch-hop	Synthwave
Dub	Hardcore	Trip-hop
Electro	Hardstyle	

FutureDJs: How to DJ

FutureDJs

Stage: 9

Dictionaries

Dictionary of DJ-ing terms

Word	Definition
Accent	Another word for phrase.
Amplify	Another word for boost.
Amplitude	Another word for loudness.
Analogue	Signal that can continuously vary in frequency and amplitude. Analogue equipment produces analogue signal.
Attenuate	Another word for cut.
Backbeat	A term used in electronic music to describe accenting the second and fourth beats of a bar.
Bassline	A melody or pattern of notes played by a low-pitched component of a track.
Beat-matching	The process of bringing the tempo of one track in line with the tempo of another.
BPM	The tempo marking that indicates the number of beats per minute.
Clipping	The effect on audio signal when it distorts. A waveform that is unable to reach its natural peak is 'clipped'.
Cueing	Setting the starting point of a track and readying it for playback.
DAW	A digital audio workstation like Ableton used to produce or perform music.
Decibels (Db)	Unit of measurement for amplitude/volume level.
Digital	Signal created by a series of 0s and 1s (binary).
Distortion	Unwanted sound created when signal levels are too high and it 'clips', or an effect purposefully applied to create a dirty, gritty sound.
Effects	Methods of modifying sounds through the use of music technology.
Equalisation (EQ)	Balancing the volume of frequencies within a sound.
Filter	Cuts all frequencies in a range above and/or below a specified frequency. There are three types: high-pass, low-pass and band-pass.
Frequency	The pitch of a sound, measured in Hertz (Hz).
Genre	A category of music such as trance, house, grime or Jazz. Each genre is classified by its specific attributes and traits.
Groove	The rhythmic feel of a track. The term originates from the 'groove' on a vinyl record.
Hertz (Hz)	Unit of measurement for frequency.
Hook	The hook is the repeated, catchy rhythmic or melodic idea that often includes a sample – the riff that goes around and around in your head.

In sync	When two tracks are aligned and at the same tempo.
Input device	The devices that read and process the sound from a storage device (CDJ, turntable, laptop).
Levels	The volume of signal as shown by meters at various stages in the signal flow.
Looping	Continually repeating a defined section of a track.
Meters	Visual indicators of signal volume at different stages in the signal flow.
MIDI	The standard for connecting electronic musical instruments to computers. MIDI files carry performance information rather than audio information.
Mix	A selection of tracks that have been mixed together into one uninterrupted string of music.
Mixer	A device that is used to blend the levels of incoming sounds together and output them as a combined audio signal.
Monitoring	The process of listening to sound through headphones or speakers.
Mono	A single audio channel with no separate Left and Right information.
Off-beat	A rhythm that falls in-between the main beats.
Output device	The piece of equipment the signal goes to once it has left the mixer. This may include amplifiers, speakers or recording devices.
Pan	Short for 'panorama'. Controlling the position of a sound between the Left and Right channels.
Phrase	A musical sentence.
Pulse	The regular, steady beat of music, like your heart beat. The length of each beat always stays the same.
Quantise	A feature that allows sounds to be snapped to the beat or fraction of the beat.
Riff	A repeated pattern or melody.
Sampler	An electronic musical instrument that allows you to change and compose with prerecorded sounds.
Scratching	A DJ-ing technique that creates sound by moving a record or sample back and forth under the needle while opening and closing the crossfader. It can be replicated on a digital set-up, using digital files and a jog wheel.
Section	A part of a track containing the same or similar characteristics.
Signal flow	The path of electrical current through equipment and set-ups.
Sound waves	Waves of vibrating particles created by sound.
Stereo	Audio with both Left and Right channels.
Storage device	USB stick, CD, vinyl record, and so on.
Synthesizer	An electronic musical instrument that creates sound through a combination of oscillators which make waveforms that can be shaped using filters and other parameters.
Transition	The process of changing from one track to another.

Dictionary of musical terms

Word	Definition
A cappella	Unaccompanied singing.
Bar	A segment of time specified by a number of beats.
Chord	Two or more notes played at the same time.
Cross-rhythm	Rhythms that do not fit well together that are played at the same time e.g. a straight beat against a triplet beat.
Dominant	The chord built on the 5th note of the scale.
Dynamics	Changes in volume.
Harmony	The combination of notes and chords.
Improvisation	Music made up and performed without a pre-prepared plan.
Instrumental	Music performed by instruments, without vocals.
Key	A group of specific pitches linked to a scale. The group is named after the first note in the scale.
Major	Music in a major key usually sounds happy and upbeat.
Major chord	A chord that has a positive/happy sound. The chord of C major contains the notes C E G.
Minor	Music in a minor key usually sounds sad and dark.
Minor chord	A chord that has a sad sound. The chord of C minor contains the notes C E♭ G.
Modulation	Changing key in the middle of a track.
Monophonic	A single unaccompanied musical line. The Minimoog is a monophonic synthesiser, because it can only play one note at a time.
Note	A specific pitch played by an instrument or sung.
Ostinato	A short repeated musical idea. Another word for riff.
Polyphonic	Two or more independent lines playing simultaneously. The Yamaha DX7 is a polyphonic synthesiser, because you can play more than one (up to 32) notes at the same time.
Rhythm	The placement of long and short sounds relative to the pulse.
Riff	A repeated pattern or melody.
Scale	A pattern of tones and semitones, usually major or minor.
Subdominant	The chord built on the 4th note of the scale.

Syncopation	A rhythm that falls in-between the main beats.
Tempo	The speed of a track.
Texture	The relationship between different layers of sound.
Timbre	The quality and type of sound.
Time signature	The number of beats in a bar. Most electronic music has 4 beats in a bar, so is in 4/4.
Tonic	The chord built on the 1st note of the scale.
Triplet	Three notes played in the time of two.

Notes

Notes

Notes